KID MUSICIANS

TRUE TALES OF CHILDHOOD FROM

ENTERTAINERS, SONGWRITERS, AND STARS

STORIES BY *ROBIN STEVENSON*   ILLUSTRATIONS BY *ALLISON STEINFELD*

HARRY STYLES

STEVIE WONDER

DOLLY PARTON

YO-YO MA

KID MUSICIANS

TRUE TALES OF CHILDHOOD FROM

ENTERTAINERS, SONGWRITERS, AND STARS

STORIES BY *ROBIN STEVENSON*   ILLUSTRATIONS BY *ALLISON STEINFELD*

PRINCE   TAYLOR SWIFT

PAUL MCCARTNEY

BEYONCÉ

Library of Congress Cataloging-in-Publication Data
Names: Stevenson, Robin, 1968- author. | Steinfeld, Allison, illustrator.
Title: Kid musicians : true tales of childhood from entertainers, songwriters, and stars / stories by Robin Stevenson ; illustrations by Allison Steinfeld.
Description: Philadelphia, PA : Quirk Books, 2024. | Series: Kid legends ; 10 | Includes bibliographical references and index. | Audience: Ages 8–12 |
Summary: "Childhood biographies of sixteen musicians, including pop songwriters, classical performers, and R&B singers"—Provided by publisher.
Identifiers: LCCN 2023047224 (print) | LCCN 2023047225 (ebook) | ISBN 9781683693918 (hardcover) | ISBN 9781683693925 (ebook)
Subjects: LCSH: Child musicians—Biography—Juvenile literature. | LCGFT: Biographies.
Classification: LCC ML3929 B .K54 2024 (print) | LCC ML3929 B (ebook) | DDC 780.83—dc23/eng/20231016
LC record available at https://lccn.loc.gov/2023047224
LC ebook record available at https://lccn.loc.gov/2023047225

ISBN: 978-1-68369-391-8

Printed in China

Typeset in Bell MT Pro, Bulldog Std, Bulmer MT Std, and Linowrite

Designed by Paige Graff
Illustrations by Allison Steinfeld
Production management by Mandy Sampson

Quirk Books
215 Church Street
Philadelphia, PA 19106
quirkbooks.com

10 9 8 7 6 5 4 3 2 1

To Kai, David, Genevieve, and Quentin
May your lives be filled with music

Table of Contents

Introduction

D o you sing along to your favorite songs or enjoy putting on shows with your friends? Maybe you play a musical instrument or think you might like to learn how to someday. Whether you make music or just love hearing it, one thing is for sure: music is an essential part of life for people all over the world.

Music can make us want to dance. It can inspire us to create art or motivate us to run faster. It can allow us to express our feelings, helping us cry when we are sad and adding to our pleasure and sense of belonging when we come together to celebrate.

There are so many different kinds of music to listen to and learn about: classical, jazz, rhythm and blues, reggae, country, pop, hip-hop, and many more! And music is always changing, as each new generation of musicians learns from the lessons and legacies of those that came before them, building on the innovations of the past to create their own unique sounds.

The musicians in this book composed, sang, played, and performed in ways that pushed boundaries and changed the world of music. Today, they are all famous—but of course, they were once kids, too.

Some of these musicians started learning their craft at an early age. When Mariah Carey was just a toddler, she used to listen to her opera singer mother practicing her scales. Yo-Yo Ma's father began teaching him the cello when he was three years old.

Many of them knew they would be musicians when they were still children. A young Prince told his teacher that he was going to be a rock-and-roll star, and eleven-year-old Cher spent hours practicing her signature for when she became famous. Still, other people didn't necessarily believe these future musicians. When Dolly Parton announced that she was going to Nashville to become a country singer, her classmates laughed at her.

Childhood was difficult for some of these musicians. In New Orleans, little Louis Armstrong dropped out of school at age eleven and learned to play trumpet in a reform school. Growing up in the 1950s, singers Diana Ross and Stevie Wonder often faced racism and discrimination. And in the Canadian prairies, singer-songwriter Joni Mitchell spent months in the hospital battling polio.

Some of these musicians were very poor before they became successful. Reggae artist Bob Marley found himself homeless at age seventeen, and singer Ella Fitzgerald lived on the streets for a time until she won a talent contest as a teenager.

But no matter how great their talent or how challenging the obstacles in their paths, all of these musicians started out as kids who loved to play and be creative. Stevie Wonder rode on a bicycle with his brother, Harry Styles liked dressing up in a dalmatian costume, and Taylor Swift invented imaginative stories on her family's Christmas tree farm. Classical pianist

Glenn Gould loved animals so much that he even made a newspaper for his pets!

These musicians pursued their dreams and made music that has touched the lives of millions of people around the world. Many of them inspired each other! Ella Fitzgerald used to imitate Louis Armstrong's singing, Mariah Carey was a big fan of Stevie Wonder, Beyoncé studied the musical careers of Diana Ross and Prince, and Taylor Swift's first demo tape included songs by Dolly Parton.

Through music, people are able to communicate feelings and ideas—which means that songs can bring people together and help make big changes in the world we live in. Music has formed the soundtrack for movements towards civil rights, social justice, and world peace.

All the musicians in this book have created music that has enriched our world. We hope their stories and music will enrich your life, too.

PART

ONE

DREAMERS TO POP SUPERSTARS

★ ★ ★ **OVERCOMING** ★ ★ ★

OBSTACLES
AND DEFYING
THE ODDS,
THESE
YOUNG MUSICIANS
SANG THEIR WAY
TO THE TOP
★ ★ ★ OF THE ★ ★ ★
MUSIC CHARTS.

Cher

Grown-up and Famous

Cher's musical career has spanned more than sixty years. She has had a hit song in every decade since the 1960s. Even as a little kid, she knew she wanted to be famous.

Cher's mother, Jackie Jean Crouch, was born in Arkansas and grew up in poverty. After moving to Los Angeles with her father, she met an Armenian American man named John Sarkisian. The young couple were still in their teens when they married and moved to El Centro, a small town in California. John's father bought him five trucks so that he could start his own produce business, harvesting and delivering watermelons.

A year after their wedding, their daughter, Cherilyn, was born on May 20, 1946. Jackie and John's relationship had been rocky from the start—and when John lost all his trucks by gambling, the produce business idea fell apart. The couple divorced before their daughter's first birthday, and Jackie took her baby and moved to a neighborhood close to Hollywood. Jackie changed her name to Georgia, and she held down various jobs while pursuing an acting career.

Because she needed to work, Cher's mom left her daughter in a Catholic children's home—a kind of orphanage that doubled as a day care facility. Georgia visited Cher at the children's home every day—but still, it was a confusing time for the little girl.

Cher's grandmothers helped look after her, but Cher was often lonely. She invented two imaginary friends, Sam and Pete, who were very real to her: "They were both truck drivers," Cher explained, "although Pete looked more like a lumberjack to me, with his black-and-red-checked shirt and hat with flappy things over the ears." Cher had tea parties with them, with three cups and a teapot filled with lemonade.

When Cher was four years old, she went to see the movie *Dumbo* at a movie theater on Hollywood Boulevard. It was a magical experience for her: the huge screen, the color film, the animated animals singing and dancing. She couldn't tear her eyes away—even when she realized that she needed to go to the restroom! "I didn't want to miss a second of *Dumbo*. I made a conscious decision: I just wasn't going to get up from my seat," she said. "So I peed in my pants."

Cher's mom, Georgia, remarried, and she and her new husband, John Southall, had another child, named Georganne. When the baby arrived, Cher was not impressed—Georganne cried a lot, and no one paid any attention to Cher—but soon she grew attached to her new sister. One day she picked out some of her own toys for Georganne to play with. Unfortunately, the baby pulled the tiny wheels off Cher's favorite little blue car—and swallowed them! Panicked, their parents called the doctor. Georganne was fine—but Cher was sent to her room! She said it was just the first of many times her little sister got her in trouble.

Even as a little kid, Cher loved music. At age three, she danced around the house naked, singing at the top of her lungs. After seeing the movie *Cinderella* as a five-year-old, she amazed her mother by singing one of the songs in the car on the way home. "I could hear a song once and remember every word," she said. Cher loved listening to her mom's albums of Broadway musicals and putting on shows for her mom and Georganne—or just for herself, turning up the volume on the record player and singing and dancing in the living room when no one else was home.

Because Cher's family moved often, she attended many different schools, and through all the change she fell further and further behind the other students. She later learned that she had dyslexia, a learning disability that makes reading slower and more difficult, but as a kid, she just knew that she couldn't keep up with the class or finish her homework. "I'd sit in class and daydream about the movies we'd seen the night before," she said.

At home, life was complicated. Her mom and her stepfather often fought, and sometimes John became violent. This was frightening and upsetting for Cher, who would hide in her room, being as quiet as possible. "I hated those fights," she said. When she was nine years old, Georgia and John separated. Cher missed her stepfather, but she didn't miss the fighting: "I was so sad about it . . . but I knew we were better off without him," she said.

Cher, Georganne, and their mom moved to a new home in the San Fernando Valley. After living in many apartments, this was the first time Cher lived in a house, and she loved it. She and Georganne shared a bedroom that their mom wallpapered just for them: pale blue, with butterflies. In their neighborhood there were lots of kids to play with, and big backyards to have fun in. "All us kids ran around like wild banshees," Cher said; it was "a child's paradise."

The house had two fruit trees in the front yard—one peach and one apricot. On Cher's and Georganne's birthdays, their mom would hang balloons from one tree and lollipops from the other!

Cher had always loved performing, and in fifth grade, she found a way to bring her love of performing to school: she produced a performance of the musical *Oklahoma!*. She organized a group of girls, directing and choreographing their dance routines. The musical had parts for male singers too, but the boys in her class refused to take part. That didn't stop Cher; she acted all the male roles and sang all their songs herself.

By the time she turned eleven, Cher had a goal. "I didn't know how or what I was going to do but I knew that I wanted to be famous," she said. She spent many hours practicing her autograph!

That year, something surprising happened: Cher's mom asked if she wanted to meet her biological father. Cher had always considered her stepfather to be her dad, and even though he and her mom were no longer together, she still saw him occasionally—but she hadn't seen John Sarkisian since she was a baby! She was curious, so she agreed to meet him. When Cher first saw him, she noticed that he had the same smile as her, and that they shared the same dark hair and eyes. He seemed nice, but he felt like a stranger to her. "He was just a man who'd walked into our house with my smile," she said.

Over the next few years, Cher went to many different schools, but she didn't much like any of them. In junior high, she went to a Catholic boarding school in Burbank, California. It was very strict, with a lot of rules, and she and the other students wore uniforms to class. Cher had packed jeans and shorts to wear when she changed out of her uniform at the end of the school day, but the nuns who ran the school said those weren't allowed. The only dress she'd brought was a pink one, and for the first week she had to wear it every day after school. This earned her the nickname Pinky.

At age fourteen, Cher briefly attended Fresno High School, but she soon transferred to a private school in Encino called Montclair College Preparatory School. Her classmates were from wealthy families, and Cher found it difficult to fit in. Because of her dyslexia, reading and writing were still a struggle, so everything she learned, she learned by listening. She often daydreamed about the future. Looking back, she said, "I was never really in school. I was always thinking about when I was grown up and famous."

When Cher was fifteen years old, her mom married again. Her new stepfather, a bank manager named Gilbert LaPiere, adopted Cher and Georganne. Officially, Cher's name became Cherilyn LaPiere. "I went by different last names as a child, but none of them seemed really me," she said. "And no one ever called me by my real first name. It was always 'Cher.'"

A year later, just three weeks into eleventh grade, Cher quit going to school. Her parents said she couldn't just sit around the house, and they helped her to sign up for acting classes. Cher was much younger than the other students, who were all adults, but she loved it. It was, she said, a turning point for her. "At last I was good at something," she said. "I could make people feel."

Later that same year, Cher met a man named Sonny Bono. He was a decade older than Cher and working as a singer and songwriter, and he was looking for a housekeeper. Cher needed a place to live, so she moved in and began working for him. Neither of them could have predicted that just three years later, they would be married, performing together, and rising to fame! Their 1965 hit song—"I Got You Babe"—reached number one on music charts in both the United States and the UK. Sonny and Cher also hosted a television show together, *The Sonny and Cher Comedy Hour.* Cher had struggled with stage fright in the past, but this new collaboration helped her to overcome her fears and gain the confidence to launch her career as a solo artist.

Since then, Cher has released many more hits, and songs such as "If I Could Turn Back Time," "Believe," and "Strong Enough" shot to the top of the music charts. Cher has sold more than one hundred million records, making her one of the best-selling music artists in the world. She has also won an Academy Award, an Emmy Award, and three Golden Globes for her acting!

But Cher's fame goes beyond her skill as a musician and actor: she is equally famous for her legendary sense of style, her charismatic personality, and her fearless self-expression. She has used her platform and her wealth to support many causes that are important to her—advocating for AIDS research, supporting LGBTQ+ rights, and drawing attention to the impact of the COVID-19 pandemic on the most vulnerable.

In 2010, Cher was given the honor of placing her handprints and footprints in cement in front of Grauman's Chinese Theatre in Hollywood—the very same theater where she had been entranced by *Dumbo* as a child. Cher achieved her childhood goal of becoming famous—and she has stayed famous for a remarkable six decades.

Beyoncé

Pretty Darn Perfect

Beyoncé—sometimes referred to as Queen Bey by her fans—has received more awards than any other female musical artist in history. She's also one of the best-selling musicians of all time! But as a little kid, she was very shy—until she stepped onstage.

Beyoncé's first name came from the maiden name of her mother, Tina, who was born Celestine Ann Beyoncé. Tina's parents were from Louisiana and were Creole, or French-speaking people of French, African, Spanish, and Native American descent.

Beyoncé's middle name, Giselle, was chosen by her father, Mathew Knowles. Mathew grew up in Alabama, one of seven kids in a very poor family. After graduating from college, he moved to Houston, where he met Tina.

Tina and Mathew's first child, Beyoncé Giselle Knowles, was born in Houston on September 4, 1981. As a small child, Beyoncé spent a lot of time at her mother's new business, Headliners Hair Salon. She chatted with customers and helped sweep up the hair from the floor. When Beyoncé was four years old, her little sister, Solange, was born.

Beyoncé began first grade at St. Mary's Montessori, a Catholic school in Houston. Her early school years were difficult, and other kids picked on her, teasing her about her unusual name, her light skin, and her ears: "I looked like I had big Dumbo ears," she said. All the teasing made her feel shy, so she often played alone— and then she was picked on for that, too.

Beyoncé often came home from school crying, which worried her mother. Tina decided to sign her up for dance classes, hoping it might help Beyoncé make friends. One day, her dance instructor, Darlette Johnson, was singing a song when Beyoncé joined in. Darlette couldn't believe how well the little girl sang! When Beyoncé's parents came to pick her up, Darlette persuaded them to allow Beyoncé to take part in a community talent show.

At the performance Beyoncé sang John Lennon's song "Imagine" while her parents watched with pride. The audience gave her a standing ovation. Many of the other kids in the competition were twice Beyoncé's age, but she won first place. It was the first time she had ever stood onstage in front of an audience, and she loved the feeling it gave her. Her dad decided to enter her in more local talent shows and beauty pageants— and Beyoncé won again and again.

When she was eight years old, Beyoncé became the youngest member of a new music group called Girls Tyme. The five girls in the group rapped, danced, and sang. Denise Seals, one of the group's managers, remembered Beyoncé as a fast learner who was never afraid to ask questions. "At the age of eight, she wanted to know all there was to know about singing," Denise said. Beyoncé also liked to take charge! Denise described walking into rehearsal one day and hearing Beyoncé talking to the other girls as if she was the group's coach: "'You sing this part,' she was saying to one of them. 'Then you sing this part,' she said to another. 'If y'all do it right, it'll be harmony. But if y'all do it wrong, it'll be terrible.'"

Now you come in!

The girls spent a lot of time in rehearsals: "Someone told me in school that practice makes perfect," Beyoncé said, "and I remember thinking . . . 'Well, we must be pretty darn perfect by now, 'cause we sure have practiced enough!'" But she didn't mind. "Singing with your best friends, there's nothing better when you're a little kid. Every day felt like summer vacation."

At school, though, she was less happy. By fourth grade, she was attending a magnet school for kids who were interested in music, but it wasn't going smoothly. Beyoncé had signed up for the school choir, but then lost interest. She wanted to sing and perform as an individual, not as part of a huge group where her voice would hardly be heard. On top of this, Beyoncé was so busy practicing and performing that she didn't always do her homework.

Over the next few years, Beyoncé attended three different schools, but she never really felt like she belonged at any of them. She felt more at home with Girls Tyme, or sitting quietly on her own writing song lyrics. Her little sister, Solange, decided she wanted to be a singer as well and began carrying a notebook everywhere so she could write songs, too.

When Beyoncé was nine, she took some big steps toward building a career in music. She went to a recording studio for the first time to record two songs with Girls Tyme—and she and the rest of the group headed to California for a talent convention, to perform in front of record company executives. It was the first time Beyoncé had been on a plane, which was exciting. Still, she had one big worry. "What if I get scared and forget my words?" she asked her dad. He reminded her that he'd be right there in the front row, so she could look at him. "And if you forget the words," he told her, "just act like you're at home writing a song and just make up any old words. The audience, they don't know the difference." Beyoncé laughed and gave him a hug. The group's performance was a hit, and they got a standing ovation.

As Beyoncé became increasingly successful, her father decided he wanted to help manage her career. Girls Tyme began having practices at Beyoncé's house—in the big family room at first, and then on a large wooden deck Mathew had built for the girls to use as a stage. "We would go in the backyard and practice all day," Beyoncé said. Mathew talked to the girls about their songs, encouraging them to think about the meaning of the lyrics. They worked on their singing, their choreography, their fitness, and their teamwork.

Beyoncé's family had an apartment over the garage and the girls used to have sleepover parties there, playing games such as truth or dare in the middle of the night. When one member of the group, Kelly Rowland, thought she might have to leave the group to move to Atlanta with her mom, Beyoncé's family invited her to live with them. She ended up staying throughout her teen years, becoming like a sister to Beyoncé.

When Beyoncé was eleven, Girls Tyme had the chance to take part in *Star Search*—a televised talent program like *American Idol*—in Orlando, Florida. As the lead singer of the song they were performing, Beyoncé was nervous. She repeated the advice her dad had given her, turning it into a rhyme: do your best and let the audience do the rest. Unfortunately, the group's performance didn't go well, and their competition—an adult rock band—was far more experienced. Backstage after the performance, the girls were in tears. They weren't used to losing! But the next day, they went to Disney World, which cheered them up.

Soon after this, Mathew decided to quit his job to support his daughter's career full-time. Tina also spent a lot of time with Beyoncé and the other girls in the group, often bringing them to work with her. They practiced by performing for the customers at Headliners Salon, trying out their routines and collecting tips from the customers. Beyoncé used her money to buy a season pass to Six Flags—she loved roller coasters!

Over the next couple of years, Girls Tyme went through a lot of changes. Some members were cut from the group, which was upsetting for Beyoncé; the adults in charge were making business decisions about a music group, but the young performers saw one another as friends. The group's name changed as well—from Girls Tyme to Somethin' Fresh, to Cliché, to the Dolls, and then to Destiny. One day, a message over the school loudspeakers called Kelly and Beyoncé to the school office. For a minute, Beyoncé thought she was in trouble and wondered what she'd done wrong. But when she got to the office, her dad was there with big news: the girls had a record deal!

Beyoncé was thrilled, but that excitement didn't last long. Before the group was able to release an album, they were dropped by the record company. To make things worse, Beyoncé's family had been counting on the income that they would have earned from the record. They were now in financial difficulties and had to sell their house.

By the time Beyoncé was a teenager, she was completely focused on her musical goals. "My energy went into Destiny's Child and the dream of us getting a record deal and becoming musicians," she said.

When she was thirteen, Beyoncé spent so many hours in the studio that she injured her vocal cords, straining them from overuse. She was scared that she might have permanently damaged her voice. What if this was the end of her career? But she followed her doctor's advice and rested her voice for a whole summer, and she made a full recovery.

With her single-minded focus on her music career, it was difficult to find time for classes and homework. In ninth grade, Beyoncé left school and studied with tutors at home. This gave her more time to practice, perform, and write new songs as well. She was also interested in learning about the music industry; she had read about musicians who had come before her—artists like Diana Ross and Prince—and about how they had been influenced by those who came before them.

Despite the ups and downs, Beyoncé didn't give up—and eventually, the girls got a new contract and began recording their first album. They changed their name again, becoming Destiny's Child, and in 1998 they released their debut album. A year later, when their second album came out, they shot to the top of the charts, winning two Grammy Awards for their song

"Say My Name" and selling more than fifteen million copies of the album worldwide.

By 2003, when Beyoncé released her first album as a solo artist, she was already a star. Over the next two decades, she released one hit after another, and some of her songs are among the best-selling singles of all time. She has earned thirty-two Grammy Awards and eighty-eight Grammy nominations—more than any other singer in history! She has also won more MTV Video Music Awards than any other artist. In 2018, the BBC named her the most powerful woman in music.

Harry Styles

> Such a Thrill

As a teenager, Harry Styles rocketed to fame with the boy band One Direction. Today, he is a celebrated solo artist—but his first onstage success as a musician was in his high school's Battle of the Bands competition!

Harry Styles was born on February 1, 1994, in Redditch, England. In fact, he was nearly born in his parents' car, but they made it to the hospital just in time! Harry's parents, Anne and Desmond Styles—Des, for short—already had one child, a three-year-old girl named Gemma. When Harry was a baby, the family moved north to the village of Holmes Chapel in Cheshire, not far from the city of Manchester. There, Des got a job working for a bank. With two children under four, Anne decided that she would stay home to focus on raising the kids.

A puppy soon joined the family; Max was a speckled gray mutt, with eyes of different colors. When Harry was a toddler, he used to lie on the floor with Max and try to put his pacifier in the dog's mouth.

When Harry was five years old, he started going to Hermitage Primary School. It was close to his home, and he and Gemma walked there each morning with their mother. Harry liked entertaining people and making them laugh, so he made friends easily. At home, he and Gemma often played together. In one of Gemma's favorite games, she pretended to be a teacher, and Harry would be her student, filling in her worksheets and answering her roll call with different voices for all of the imaginary students.

Like most siblings, they also fought sometimes—like when Gemma told Harry that the WWF wrestling on the television was all just acting and not real. Harry was furious, and to get back at his sister, he told their mother that Gemma was a drug dealer. He wanted to get her in trouble, and it was the worst thing he could think of! Their mom couldn't help laughing. "No, she isn't, Harry," she said. "She's nine."

When Harry was six, he played the lead part in a Christmas musical, wearing a headband with mouse ears and a pair of his sister's tights. He loved dressing up, and luckily, his mom liked making costumes. Once she made a giant papier-mâché mug and painted an atlas on it so Harry could dress up as the World Cup. But his favorite was his dalmatian costume, which was a hand-me-down from close family friends.

Harry loved performing and being onstage, and he rarely felt shy. As he grew older, he enjoyed singing and acting in school plays. In class, though, his love of entertaining people sometimes caused problems. Harry often got in trouble for joking around, talking in class, and distracting other kids.

When Harry was seven, his parents sat him and Gemma down to tell them some sad news: they were getting divorced. Soon after that, Des moved out, and Harry and Gemma continued to live in the house with their mom, spending time with their father on the weekends. Harry's parents hadn't been happy together, but they both loved their children very much.

When Harry was nine, his mom married John Cox, the landlord of a local pub. Anne and John decided to take over another pub and run it together—they and the kids would live upstairs. Harry became best friends with a boy named Reg, who lived nearby. In the summers they went for bike rides together, exploring the countryside and always stopping for ice cream cones on the way home.

Harry started taking guitar lessons when he was ten, from one of the pub's regular customers who had once been in a rock band. But music wasn't a big part of his life yet. His main interests were sports: badminton, which his dad played, and soccer (which is called football in England). Harry joined a soccer team and played every weekend. He wasn't a great player—in fact, the one time he played goalie his team lost 8–0—but he always enjoyed spending time with his friends and joking around with the spectators.

After three years of marriage, Anne and John split up and the pub was sold. The new owners were the parents of Harry's good friend Reg! Anne bought a three-bedroom house for herself, Gemma, and Harry to live in, and Harry started high school at Holmes Chapel Comprehensive School. After school, he often went to his friend Will's house for pizza and fries.

As a young teen, Harry was also busy working at a bakery. He helped open the store early in the morning, packed up orders, stocked the shelves, and cleaned the floors. He was good at the job and always greeted the customers with a smile. He also enjoyed the treats he got there; the owner, Simon, made delicious pasties, handmade pies filled with bacon, sausage, scrambled eggs, and cheese. Harry's friend Nick worked at the bakery too.

One day while Nick was serving a customer, he heard Harry singing loudly while sweeping the floor out back. Harry hadn't realized that they had a customer in the shop! But the customer was so impressed that he told Harry to get in touch if he ever wanted to sing professionally.

When Harry was fifteen, his friends decided to start a band. Will would be the drummer, Nick would play bass, and their friend Haydn would play lead guitar. All they needed was a singer. Harry's parents had always praised his singing—his grandfather had even given him a karaoke machine—but Harry didn't think he was good enough. What if people laughed at him?

But his friends talked him into it, and the four of them entered their school's Battle of the Bands competition. For Harry, being in the band was about fashion as well as music—he wanted to look good! At the time, he and his sister were both into the emo look: studded belts, skinny jeans, and floppy hair. Harry attempted to straighten his curls. Nick suggested that that the band members should all get their ears pierced but Harry was worried his mom wouldn't approve.

At the Battle of the Bands, they performed two songs: "Summer of '69" by Bryan Adams and "Are You Gonna Be My Girl" by Jet. The crowd loved them—and they won! The prize was one hundred pounds, plus the opportunity to perform at a local music festival in a nearby village. That led to more invitations, and their band started to become popular locally, often performing songs by the Beatles and Blink-182. They even played at a wedding, learning the bride's favorite Bob Marley songs!

But Harry still wasn't counting on a career in music. He wasn't sure what he wanted to do—maybe work in business, he thought, or perhaps physical therapy, like his girlfriend, Abi, was considering. His mom encouraged him to audition for *The X Factor*—a music competition on television—and when he didn't get around to applying, she finally filled in the application form and sent it off herself! Harry was given a date for the tryouts and told to prepare two songs.

And then he practiced. He had been singing around the house for years, rehearsing for school musicals, or in his room with his karaoke machine, but now, all of a sudden, he felt shy. He sang in the bathroom with the door shut (but his mother and Gemma sat on the landing outside and listened).

Finally, it was time for the first round of auditions. More than six thousand people showed up to watch! Harry introduced himself, saying that he was from Holmes Chapel, in Cheshire: "It's quite boring," he said. "Nothing much happens there." He talked about his band, and the excitement of winning the Battle of the Bands, saying, "I got such a thrill when I was in front of people singing that it made me want to do it more and more." Then he got up on the stage and sang Stevie Wonder's song "Isn't She Lovely."

The judges voted—and two of the three said yes. Harry was moving on to the next stage of the competition! But he wasn't allowed to tell anyone; he had to keep it secret for two whole months, until it was time to head to London for the next stage in the contest, which was called boot camp.

At boot camp, Harry was eliminated. He thought that was the end of his journey with *The X Factor*, but to his surprise, he was called back along with four other contestants. They were asked if they wanted to continue in the competition—not as solo performers but as a brand-new boy band. It wasn't over after all! The boys called their group One Direction, and after placing third in *The X Factor*, they signed a record contract. They were an instant success and released five chart-topping albums in five years.

Harry struck out on his own in 2016, beginning a new career as a solo artist. The following year, his first solo album debuted at number one on both sides of the Atlantic Ocean and was one of the world's top-ten best-selling albums of the year. His third solo album received a Grammy Award for album of the year in 2023. Harry also acted in several movies and became known for his love of fashion, becoming the first man to appear solo on the cover of *Vogue* magazine. He regularly speaks out in support of gender equality and LGBTQ+ rights and has used his position to promote a message of love and acceptance, adopting the slogan TPWK, which means "Treat People with Kindness."

Taylor Swift

I Can't Wait to Be Great

Taylor Swift has explored the genres of country, folk, and pop, writing songs that tell stories and speak to the hearts of her millions of devoted fans. Before she was famous, she wrote her first songs as a little kid living on a Christmas tree farm.

Taylor Alison Swift was born in West Reading, Pennsylvania, on December 13, 1989. Her father, Scott Kingsley Swift, was an investment banker, and her mother, Andrea Gardner Swift, worked in marketing. They chose the name Taylor because they loved the music of singer-songwriter James Taylor. They also liked that it was a gender-neutral name, because they hoped this might help her avoid experiencing discrimination based in sexism.

Taylor started singing when she was just a toddler—and she always loved to have an audience. Her parents have videos of her walking up to people on the beach and singing for them. "I was literally going from towel to towel," she remembers, "saying, 'Hi, I'm Taylor. I'm going to sing "I Just Can't Wait to Be King" for you now.'"

She already had a remarkable memory for music and song lyrics. "I would come out of Disney movies and my parents used to get freaked out because I'd be singing the entire soundtrack of the movie after hearing it once," she said.

By the time she was three, Taylor could even sing difficult songs, like the Righteous Brothers' "Unchained Melody." She had also started making up her own songs by changing the words to songs she knew. Her early songwriting efforts included songs with titles like "I Love My Dolly" and "I Can't Wait to Be Great!"

This same year, Taylor's younger brother, Austin, was born. Andrea decided to take a step back from her career. She had two kids under five and she wanted to focus her time and energy on raising them.

As a child, Taylor lived on a Christmas tree farm just six miles from Reading, Pennsylvania. "It was the most magical, wonderful place in the world," Taylor said. "Having . . . the space to use your imagination and create stories and fairy tales out of everyday life—I think that had a lot to do with me wanting to write songs." Taylor even made up stories about the dead squirrels and birds that the barn cats left on the driveway.

For Taylor's parents, the farm involved a lot of work, but Taylor was free to build forts in the hay loft, play in the orchard, or take the pony out for trail rides. She did have one important job to do, though: she was responsible for picking the eggs of praying mantises off the Christmas trees. One year, she forgot to do this . . . and all over town, families found their Christmas trees covered in praying mantises as thousands of tiny eggs hatched.

There was always music playing in Taylor's home—her dad liked pop, her mom liked hard rock, and her grandmother used to be an opera singer—but it was country music that captured Taylor's imagination. By the time she was six, she had discovered country singer LeAnn Rimes and learned many of her songs by heart. She listened to Shania Twain, and as she grew older, she learned more about the history of country music, falling in love with singers such as Dolly Parton and Patsy Cline.

Country songs often told stories—and Taylor loved stories. In second grade, when the students were asked to write two sentences, Taylor wrote three pages! She also loved poetry, and when she was ten, her poem "Monster in My Closet" won a national poetry contest. "Poetry is what turned me into a songwriter," Taylor said.

When she found out that her school would be putting on a play, she was determined to play the lead part so that she could sing a solo. The character was named Freddie Fast Talk, and he was the villain of the show. Taylor didn't care: she wanted that part and she got it! She dressed up, drawing on a mustache and eyebrows and putting her hair up in a hat, and she sang her solo.

In 1999, Taylor's family left the farm and moved to Wyomissing, Pennsylvania. She began attending Wyomissing Area Junior/Senior High School, but she found it hard to fit in and make friends.

Luckily, her mom discovered a community theater group called the Berks County Youth Theatre Academy. Taylor auditioned for the show *Annie*, and was chosen to play a small part. This helped Taylor gain confidence, and she played lead roles in two more musicals: *The Sound of Music* and *Grease*.

Taylor spent her summers at her family's vacation home in Stone Harbor, New Jersey. Spending summer at the shore meant jet-skiing, swimming, and bird-watching, or going to the mall. She also loved going to the ice cream shop in town, where there were so many flavors it was almost impossible to choose.

With her brother, Austin, Taylor turned the room above the vacation house's garage into a secret clubhouse—so secret that other kids needed a password to enter! She painted the room different colors and said she could happily spend the whole day sitting in there. One summer, she wrote an entire 350-page novel in that clubhouse.

When Taylor was eleven, her friend Kaylin came to Stone Harbor with her, and the two girls decided to start a beauty products company. They collected wildflowers, ground them up, and called the resulting paste "all-natural body lotion." Unfortunately, it smelled terrible and turned brown—so the girls decided to make up dances to Spice Girls songs instead. Taylor also wrote many songs that summer, and sang for customers at the local café, Coffee Talk, and at the local seafood restaurant, Henny's.

That fall, Taylor watched a documentary about Faith Hill and decided that she needed to go to Nashville, Tennessee. Nashville, she thought, was the place where country music dreams came true. After months of begging, Taylor's mom agreed to take her on a trip. Taylor made a demo tape, singing songs by her favorite artists—Dolly Parton, LeAnn Rimes, and the Dixie Chicks—and with her mom driving her around the city, she hand-delivered copies of the homemade tape to all the record companies, hoping someone would call her and offer her a record deal.

But no one did. Taylor was only eleven years old, and Nashville was full of talented young singers who were just as good as she was. Taylor realized she needed to come up with a way to make herself stand out. Lots of people could sing—but not everyone could write their own songs, so she decided to focus on that. She also learned to play guitar. She practiced until her fingers were swollen and bleeding, and her mom would have to tape them up for her.

Her intense focus on singing and guitar didn't make Taylor popular at her middle school. Kids whispered and laughed about her behind her back, making fun of her love of country music, her shyness, and even her hair. In hopes of fitting in, Taylor tried out for the basketball team, but despite being tall, she was terrible at it. She didn't enjoy running and was a little bit uncoordinated. She preferred board games to sports. To make things worse, the theater company had closed, and she and Kaylin had drifted apart.

Music was Taylor's escape—and writing songs was a way to express herself. She began traveling to New York City for singing and acting lessons, and when she was twelve, she sang the national anthem at a basketball game in Philadelphia—to twenty thousand fans! It was her biggest show by far, but for Taylor, the highlight was when Jay-Z, who was sitting in the audience, high-fived her as she walked by.

Nice job!

When Taylor was fourteen, her parents bought a house just outside Nashville and she started at a new school. To her relief, the other students were welcoming and she soon made a good friend. Taylor's parents had decided to move to the Nashville area so that Taylor could pursue a career in music, but they made a point of telling her it was still okay if she decided on a different path. But Taylor had no intention of changing her mind! She was always writing songs, often recording a melody by humming it into her phone or scribbling lyrics in the margins of her schoolwork.

Taylor was just sixteen when her first album catapulted her into the spotlight. It was a blend of country and pop music, and the songs were inspired by her own teenage experiences. She promoted it online, using the social media platform MySpace, which helped her to reach a young audience and begin building a relationship with the many adoring fans who would later come to be known as Swifties. Her album shot to the top of the charts—but she was just getting started.

Today, Taylor may be the world's biggest pop star. She has broken dozens of world records for the number of music awards she has received and for her album sales and chart-topping hit songs. In 2023, Taylor embarked on her Eras tour, performing more than 150 shows across five continents. She broke records for ticket sales—and the movie documenting her tour broke yet more records, becoming the highest earning concert film of all time. All around the world, people were listening to Taylor: she was named Spotify's Global

Top Artist for 2023, with more than 26 billion streams.

Taylor has also been a powerful advocate for the rights of artists in the music industry. You might notice that some of her songs are labeled as "Taylor's Version." That's because she rerecorded her early albums in order to reclaim the ownership of these songs from her former record company. She has been an outspoken supporter of LGBTQ+ rights, declaring her shows a safe and celebratory space while criticizing harmful laws and encouraging people to vote for candidates who stand up for equality. And she's earned some high praise from one of her childhood idols. "She knew exactly who she was, she had her dream, and she stuck with it," Dolly Parton said of Taylor. "That's what you gotta do. I'm just so proud of her."

One of the world's biggest music trends of the last decade is K-pop, or Korean pop music! Leading the trend is a group of seven talented young performers: BTS, also known as the Bangtan Boys, are famous for their hip-hop-inspired music, high-energy performances, and striking outfits. With catchy lyrics that speak directly to young people, they have won millions of fans around the world.

BTS believes that music can bring people together and create a world where everyone feels seen, heard, and valued. Their fans agree! Calling themselves BTS ARMY—ARMY stands for Adorable Representative M.C. for Youth—they have an online community of over forty million members.

BTS has taken their message of love and acceptance around the world. They've spoken at the United Nations and visited President Joe Biden at the White House to discuss anti-Asian hate crimes and discrimination. In 2019, *Time* magazine included BTS on their list of the 100 most influential people in the world.

TWO

JAZZ CLUBS AND CONCERT HALLS

★ ★ **FROM THE STREETS OF** ★ ★

NEW ORLEANS

TO THE STAGES OF

NEW YORK CITY,

these

KID MUSICIANS

pursued

THEIR PASSIONS

★ ★ ★ **AND CHANGED** ★ ★ ★

THE MUSICAL LANDSCAPE

FOREVER.

Louis Armstrong

Little Louis

ouis Armstrong is known as the father of jazz. A skilled trumpeter, he turned his voice into a second instrument, inspiring a new approach to singing that had a huge influence on other musicians. He grew up poor but was always surrounded by music.

Louis Armstrong was born in New Orleans on August 4, 1901. His parents, William Armstrong and Mary Estelle Albert, who was known as Mayann, were very young when they had him; Mayann was just fifteen years old. When Louis was still a baby, they split up, and both of them moved away, leaving Louis with his grandmother. They later reunited for a short time and had a baby girl named Beatrice—but Louis wouldn't meet his sister until he was five years old.

Louis's grandmother was named Josephine Armstrong, and she lived in a poor Black neighborhood in New Orleans. This part of the city was called Storyville or Back o' Town, but it was widely known as the Battlefield, because, Louis said, "the toughest characters in town used to live there." There was lots of drinking, and lots of fighting and crime, but it was home to Louis: "I loved all those people and they loved me," he said. "The good ones and the bad ones all thought that Little Louis (as they called me) was okay."

Josephine sent Louis to church and Sunday school. "That, I guess, is how I acquired my singing tactics," he said. "At church my heart went into every hymn I sang." When Josephine cleaned houses and did laundry for white families, she'd bring Louis along and give him a nickel for his help. "I thought I was rich!" he remembered. Those early years were good ones for Louis, who loved his grandmother very much.

One day, when Louis was five years old, a woman he'd never seen before showed up at his grandmother's house. Louis's mother was sick, she said, and needed

Louis to help take care of her and Beatrice, who was now a toddler. Louis's grandmother was sad to let him go, but she agreed that he should help his mother. Promising he'd come back, Louis headed off with the stranger to catch the trolley. He couldn't help crying. The woman pointed at the nearby prison, called the House of Detention. "If you don't stop crying at once I will put you in that prison," she said. Louis was terrified.

When Louis arrived at the room where his mother, Mayann, was lying sick in bed, he finally met his sister, Beatrice, who was known by the nickname Mama Lucy. Mayann gave Louis some money and told him to buy some food. When he returned, the room was full of people he'd never seen before. There were seven kids there—and they were all his cousins!

Their dad, Louis's uncle Ike Miles, became an important person in young Louis's life. Louis's mother would often disappear for days at a time, leaving him with Uncle Ike and the cousins. They shared a single room: "He put as many in the bed as it would hold and the rest slept on the floor," Louis remembered.

Louis began kindergarten at the Fisk School, not far from his home. He made friends easily, and was a quick learner. "I could read the newspaper to the older folk in my neighborhood," he said.

Louis also sold newspapers to make extra money for his family. Sometimes he and the older boys in the neighborhood gambled their earnings, playing dice or blackjack. On good days, Louis would come home with pockets full of coins.

When Louis was six or seven, he was hired by the Karnofskys, a family of Lithuanian Jewish immigrants who ran a nearby tailor shop. Louis worked with the family's sons, driving around on their junk and coal wagons and blowing tin horns to attract customers. This was Louis's first introduction to blowing a horn! The Karnofskys treated him like family, often inviting him to family meals, and they became an important part of his life.

Louis also found time to play with other kids in the neighborhood, running around barefoot, in and out of empty houses that were waiting to be torn down. They often played a game they called War, and one day while Louis was pretending to look for wounded comrades on the imaginary battlefield, a piece of slate fell off a roof and landed on his head. Louis was knocked out cold— but luckily, he wasn't badly hurt.

There was music everywhere in New Orleans when Louis was growing up. There was music playing at events like Mardi Gras and Carnival. There were funeral processions with brass bands. And there were bars known as honky-tonks, where musicians played ragtime music and people danced. "At the corner of the street where I lived was the famous Funky Butt Hall," Louis said. Its real name was Union Sons Hall, although no one called it that. Kids weren't allowed to go inside, but the band would come outside and play to draw in more customers. Louis and his friends would gather to listen and dance, and when the band went back inside, they'd watch through the big cracks in the wall.

When he was eleven, Louis dropped out of school and formed a quartet with three other boys. Together, they sang and danced on the streets, passing a hat for tips. The week between Christmas and New Year's Day was filled with celebrations, and one tradition involved setting off fireworks or shooting pistols into the air: "anything loud to make as much noise as possible," Louis said. So, on New Year's Eve, when Louis found a pistol in an old trunk of Mayann's, he took it with him when he went out—and when he saw another kid shoot a gun into the air, he pulled out his pistol and did the same, shooting blanks over his head. His friends laughed, but a detective who happened to be nearby did not! Shooting a gun in public was (and is) dangerous, as well as illegal. Louis was arrested and spent the night locked in a cell.

The next morning, a man took him to a wagon pulled by two horses. "You are going to the Colored Waif's Home for Boys," the man told him. The Waif's Home was a reform school for boys who had broken the law. The building was near a dairy farm, and when Louis arrived, the first thing he saw was hundreds of cows. Inside the home, the boys were eating beans for lunch—but Louis was too sad and scared to eat. He didn't know it, but the situation could have been even worse: before this home opened in 1906, the only Waif's Homes were for white children—and Black boys who were arrested were sent to jail along with adults.

The teachers at the home were strict, but the boys had the opportunity to learn skills that interested them—including music. Mr. Davis, the music teacher, invited Louis to join the brass band. Louis played a tambourine, and then drums, and then, to his delight, a bugle. It was old, its brass tarnished green, but Louis polished it until it gleamed, and he played so well that Mr. Davis gave him a cornet—a kind of trumpet. Louis practiced hard and became so skilled that Mr. Davis made him band leader.

Music gave Louis opportunities to leave the school, playing at parades that wove through the city, wearing cream-colored pants, brown stockings, and a cap. One day, the band's parade route took them twenty-five miles! "We loved every foot of the trip," Louis said.

When he was thirteen, Louis was released from the home to live with his father, whom he barely knew. Louis was often left to look after his half brothers, Henry and Willie, while his father and stepmother worked. Louis took on the job of cooking for the family, too. He didn't mind looking after Henry, but he found Willie very difficult. "He was such a terrible liar that sometimes I wanted to throw a whole pot of beans at his head," he said. After a year of living there, Louis moved back in with his mother and sister. He worked hard, playing the blues at a honky-tonk at night and driving a coal cart during the day.

At age seventeen, Louis accepted an offer to play cornet in a dance band on board one of the steamboats that toured up and down the Mississippi River. The boat was named the SS *Sidney*, and the band, led by a jazz pianist named Fate Marable, was famous. It was there that Louis learned to read music; in fact, he referred to his time on the steamboat as "going to the University."

In 1922, Louis moved to Chicago to join King Oliver's Creole Jazz Band. He played cornet and began to sing as well. Two years later, he moved to New York City to play with the Fletcher Henderson Orchestra, finally switching to the instrument he is best known for: the trumpet.

Louis Armstrong went on to become a jazz legend,

with a career spanning more than five decades. He appeared in movies and on television, and he toured with his band, Louis Armstrong's All-Stars. He is equally famous for his trumpet playing and his voice, and many of his songs, such as "What a Wonderful World," are famous around the globe. His influence on both jazz and popular music continues to this day.

Ella Fitzgerald

Queen of Jazz

Sometimes called the First Lady of Song, Ella Fitzgerald is known as one of the greatest jazz musicians ever. She was a hugely talented singer, with a pitch-perfect voice that has been loved by millions—but when she was growing up, she imagined a future as a dancer.

Ella Jane Fitzgerald was born April 25, 1917, in Virginia. Her father, William, was a wagon driver, and her mother, Temperence, known as Tempie, worked doing laundry. They separated when Ella was still a baby, and Tempie met someone new: a Portuguese immigrant named Joseph Da Silva. Together, they moved to the city of Yonkers, New York. Like many Black Americans, they wanted to escape the poverty, segregation, and racist violence of the South.

When the family first arrived in Yonkers, with little money and no jobs, they had no choice but to move into a temporary shelter—one of twenty-eight rooms in a red brick building on Clinton Street. Soon, though, Tempie found a job at the Silver Lining Laundry and Joe began working at a sugar refinery.

In 1923, Tempie gave birth to a second child, Ella's half sister, Frances. In September of that year, Ella— now a tall six-year-old—started school. She went to Public School 10, right at the end of her block. Two years later, the family moved five blocks east, to a new home in a big apartment building on School Street. The building was in a poor neighborhood, and most of its residents were Italian, but there were a number of Black families and a few immigrants from Ireland, Greece, and Eastern Europe.

There were lots of kids living in Ella's building, and they would often play together. One of them, Charles, was the same age as Ella, and both loved to dance. They practiced dance steps in the street and begged the older kids to show them the latest moves from Harlem's ballrooms and dance halls. Charles's older sister Annette remembered how Ella and Charles used to put on shows together. "She would get up and sing and dance. . . . It was then that we'd say Ella was going to go places, as a dancer!" Ella thought so too; despite being shy sometimes, she was ambitious. "Someday you're going to see me in the headlines," Ella used to say. "I'm going to be famous!"

In fourth grade, Ella started at a new school— Public School 18—and made a new friend: an Italian girl named Rose Sarubbi, who lived just two blocks away. The two girls became very close, and Ella spent a

lot of time at Rose's home. She liked Rose's dad a lot—
and she loved the spaghetti Rose's mom cooked! The
girls stayed good friends throughout their school years.

Ella's family went to church every Sunday, and Ella
attended Sunday school there. Church provided her
with opportunities to listen to music and sing. Singing
came naturally to her—she had the ability to hear a
song on the radio and mimic the singer, hitting every
note perfectly—and by the time she started at Benjamin
Franklin Junior High School, she was known as the girl
who loved to sing and dance. One of her classmates
remembered how Ella was always dancing and singing,
even on her way to school, or standing outside at lunch:
"She just smiled all the time, just shaking her shoulders
and singing."

Ella was particularly drawn to the groundbreaking singing style of Louis Armstrong. She would sing along to his songs, learning from the way he improvised not just with his trumpet but with his voice—which is known as scat singing. She could do a remarkable imitation of him! Her friends were impressed with her ability to sing popular songs, and their enthusiasm encouraged her. At home, her mom supported her love of music, and when Tempie brought home a Boswell Sisters record, Ella was entranced by the voice of the lead singer, Connee Boswell. "I fell in love with it," she said. "I tried so hard to sound just like her."

But as much as she loved singing—and as talented as she was—Ella imagined a future as a dancer. Her childhood friend and neighbor, Charles, remembered,

"She was some dancer, oh yeah! She was a terrific dancer." As teenagers, Charles and Ella would take the trolley car to the subway station and ride the subway into New York City, heading to a Harlem dance hall called the Savoy Ballroom. They would learn all the latest dances—and then they'd go back to Yonkers to show off their new steps and teach them to the other kids. By the time she was fifteen, Ella was making a little money dancing in clubs in Yonkers on Saturday nights.

Then something shocking and sad happened: Ella's mother died suddenly. Ella left school and went to live with her aunt Virginia, Tempie's sister, in Harlem. Not long after this, Ella's stepfather, Joe, also died, and Ella's half sister, Frances, came to live with Virginia, too.

This was a very difficult time for Ella. She stopped going to school and got involved with an illegal lottery scheme to make money. When she was caught doing this, she was sent to an orphanage—but she soon ran away. When the authorities found her, they sent her to a harsh reform school for girls.

By the fall of 1934, Ella was back in Harlem. Just seventeen years old, she was on her own and living on the streets, trying to survive by singing and dancing on the corners for tips—but she was still determined to succeed in show business. When she heard about a new talent show at the Apollo Theater—a Harlem music venue that is now famous for its role in music history—she decided to enter. She had planned to dance, but when she saw that a very talented pair of dancers was competing, she decided to sing instead.

She was nervous when she got onstage—a shy and awkward teenager in a dirty dress, with no real experience performing—but when she opened her mouth to sing, the crowd went wild! They loved her, and Ella won the contest. As part of her prize, she was supposed to be given more opportunities to perform at the theater, but the Apollo management didn't like how she looked: she needed a shower, her hair was a mess, and she was wearing old clothes and men's boots. Two months later, at the Harlem Opera House, Ella won another contest—and this time, she was booked to perform for a week, playing with the Tiny Bradshaw Band.

This contest win opened a new door for her—one that would change her life. Chick Webb, the drummer and leader of the Tiny Bradshaw Band, needed a female vocalist, and Ella jumped at the opportunity. She had just turned eighteen when she began singing with Chick and his band at Harlem's Savoy Ballroom—the same club where she and her friend Charles had gone to dance just three years earlier. She recorded her first song, "Love and Kisses," in 1934.

When Ella was twenty-one, a song she cowrote, "A-Tisket, A-Tasket," became a major radio hit. The song was based on an old nursery rhyme, and it became one of the best-selling records of the decade. A year later, in 1939, Chick Webb died, and Ella took over the role of band leader, renaming the group Ella Fitzgerald and Her Famous Orchestra. She recorded nearly 150 songs with the group, and she also performed and recorded songs with another group, the Benny Goodman Orchestra.

Ella's musical career spanned nearly six decades, and for much of that time she was the most popular female jazz singer in the country. She collaborated with many other great performers, from Duke Ellington to her own childhood hero, Louis Armstrong. Ella won fourteen Grammy Awards, including the lifetime achievement award, as well as the National Medal of Arts and many other honors. During her lifetime, she sold more than forty million albums, and her popularity and influence continue today.

Ella faced racism and discrimination throughout her career—she was even stopped from boarding an airplane on her way to give a concert in Australia—but she used her talent and her fame to fight for change. In the 1950s, she hired a manager who was a civil rights activist and demanded that her shows be free of discrimination. This wasn't easy. Once, in Texas, Ella and other musicians were all arrested for putting on an integrated show in defiance of racist laws that kept white people and Black people segregated. But she kept fighting, breaking barriers for those who would follow her. Ella was awarded the 1987 NAACP President's Award for her contributions to the fight for civil rights.

Glenn Gould

Enchanted

Glenn Gould is one of the most famous classical pianists of the twentieth century, known for his brilliant interpretations of the work of Johann Sebastian Bach and for his determination to be an artist in his own way. As a child, he preferred the company of animals to being around other children.

Glenn was the only child of Russell Herbert Gold,
who was known as Bert, and Florence Emma Gold.
Bert and Florence both grew up in small towns in
Ontario, Canada, and moved to Toronto together in
1925. Bert worked as a furrier, selling fur coats in a
shop he'd inherited from his father, and Florence taught
piano. Their baby was born at home, on September 25,
1932. The name on his birth certificate was Glenn
Herbert Gold. Eight years later, after World War II
began, his parents changed their family name to Gould;
although they were not Jewish, they feared the name
Gold might make them a target of antisemitism.

Glenn was born during the Great Depression. This
was a time when many people around the world
struggled with terrible poverty, but Glenn's family was

financially secure. They lived in a part of Toronto known as the Beaches, in a middle-class home surrounded by trees. Glenn's early childhood was happy and his parents were loving. Bert said that Glenn had "a sunny disposition and a marvelous sense of humour."

When Glenn was three years old, his parents discovered he had perfect pitch, which is the remarkable ability to identify a note by hearing it. His mom, Florence, would play a chord—and from the other end of the house, Glenn would correctly identify every note!

D-sharp!

Florence started giving Glenn piano lessons when he was four years old, and he was soon making up his own songs. When he was six, she and Bert took him to his first piano recital. Years later, Glenn remembered going home in the car afterward, saying, "I was in that wonderful state of half-awakeness in which you hear all sorts of incredible sounds going through your mind. They were all orchestral sounds, but I was playing them all . . . I was enchanted."

Glenn was a sensitive child with strong likes and dislikes. He liked soft colors, like "battleship gray and midnight blue." In his mind, red was associated with violence—and when someone gave him a bright red toy fire engine, he became very upset! As an eight-year-old, he saw the Walt Disney movie *Fantasia*, and it made him feel sick and depressed and gave him a headache. He hated its "awful riot of color," he said. He preferred war movies, which tended to feature his favorite blues and grays. At school, he used to doodle battleships and submarines on his papers.

Glenn's family spent weekends and summers at a cottage on Lake Simcoe, a two-hour drive north of Toronto, where Glenn loved riding his bike, exploring the woods, and swimming in the lake. He liked going out in his boat as well, often taking his dog, and his father remembered how Glenn would return, soaking wet but happy, holding "the tiller in one hand and conducting an unseen orchestra with the other, and singing at the top of his voice."

The summer he was six, Glenn went fishing with a neighboring family. He caught a fish but became very distressed at the sight of it flopping around in the boat. "I suddenly saw this thing entirely from the fish's point of view," he said. Glenn tried to rescue the fish, but the others laughed at him and told him to sit down—so Glenn cried and screamed until they returned to shore. For the rest of that summer, he refused to talk to the neighbors.

It was the start of his lifelong opposition to cruelty to animals. He hated the idea of animals being killed for their fur, disliked when his mom wore a fur coat, and he was upset when his uncle, as a medical student, dissected a frog.

Glenn had many pets as a child—dogs, rabbits, a parakeet named Mozart, and four goldfish also named for composers: Bach, Beethoven, Haydn, and Chopin. For a while, he even had a skunk! Glenn would happily roll around on the floor playing with his dogs or let them sit beside him while he played piano. He sometimes signed cards to his mom from "Your Puppy Dog GLENN," and he would ask to be petted as if he was a dog himself. He gave his parents animal nicknames: Mouse, for his mom, and Possum, for his dad. His dog Sir Nickolson of Garelocheed—or Nicky for short—was his very best friend.

When Glenn was eight or nine, he made a newspaper for animals. *The Daily Woof* was written in pencil and reported news that might be of interest to the animals in the neighborhood. Its articles covered the thievery of a squirrel, gossip about what the neighbor's dog had been up to, stories about his

parakeet's lice, and, sadly, the death of Bach the
goldfish.

Other children were more difficult for Glenn to
relate to. "By the time I was six I'd already made an
important discovery: that I get along much better with
animals than with humans," he said. He persuaded his
parents to let him learn at home for first grade, with a
private tutor. The following year, he started second
grade at Williamson Road Public School, right behind
his family's backyard. He did not enjoy school at all.

Glenn had sloppy handwriting and although he
loved learning and found the work easy, he was careless
and messy. He skipped third grade, but this didn't make
him any happier at school. He was younger than his

classmates, and he didn't share their interest in sports. "I got along miserably with most of my teachers and all of my fellow students," he later said. He was teased, bullied, and even beaten up by other children. He became very anxious and began getting headaches and stomachaches. He worried about germs and was terrified of throwing up in public.

Piano was a comfort and a refuge. Glenn would happily practice for hours, and his parents had to encourage him to take breaks from playing; in fact, they sometimes imposed time limits, which he did not appreciate. When Glenn was seven, Florence sent him to the Toronto Conservatory of Music for piano lessons. Over the next three years, he passed the piano exams for grades 3 through 9 and earned medals for receiving the highest marks in the province.

By the time Glenn was ten, he was playing Bach's fugues, Mozart's sonatas, Chopin's waltzes, and much more. He began studying with Alberto Guerrero, who would be his teacher through his teen years. Glenn was a stubborn student who didn't like to be told what to do, and Guerrero said that even as a child, Glenn wouldn't take anyone else's word for anything. Luckily, Guerrero understood that the best way to teach Glenn was to let him discover things for himself.

Glenn's parents supported his passion for music. They even knocked down a wall in their house to build a music studio large enough to fit a second grand piano.

But they also wanted him to have a normal childhood. They allowed him to develop his musical skills at his own pace, and in his own unique ways. Sometimes he rode his bike to nearby farms and sang to the cows! He said they were a very attentive audience.

When Glenn was thirteen, he started ninth grade at Malvern Collegiate Institute. Glenn liked some of his teachers but wasn't interested in working hard at the subjects that didn't interest him. He excelled in math, and he enjoyed writing. In one English paper, the teacher gave him a failing grade, writing that he "had better things to do with his time than read papers that require one to constantly have to refer to a dictionary." Glenn couldn't resist making use of his very large vocabulary!

The other students still thought Glenn was odd—he had a tendency to conduct music or sing to himself as he walked—but he was no longer bullied. He often played piano at school assemblies and concerts, sometimes performing pieces he'd written himself. He became more confident and was happy to express his opinions; he had very strong views on many subjects, even ones he knew little about!

Glenn was only fourteen when he made his debut as a soloist with the Toronto Symphony Orchestra, and by his early twenties, he had gained worldwide recognition for his recordings of Johann Sebastian Bach's *Goldberg* Variations. He performed across North America, Europe, the Soviet Union, and Israel, but in 1964, in his early thirties, he made a decision that shocked everyone: he would no longer perform live. He said that he didn't like audiences and that concert halls were too much like sports arenas. He still worried about germs, and he hated applause!

Because Glenn most enjoyed playing when no audience was present, he decided he would focus on making studio recordings. He appreciated the technical aspects of recording music and the artistic control it gave him over the finished work. He released a number of best-selling recordings, made television and radio programs, and wrote about music and many other topics.

Glenn died in 1982, at the age of fifty. The following year he was inducted into the Canadian Music Hall of Fame. He left half of his money to the Toronto Humane Society, to help the animals he had always loved.

Yo-Yo Ma

The Big Instrument

o-Yo Ma is probably the best-known classical musician and cello player in the world—but he's also famous for his kindness, generosity, and commitment to using music to bring joy to others. He played his first concert when he was only five years old.

Yo-Yo Ma comes from a musical family. His father, Hiao-Tsiun Ma, was a violinist, composer, and professor of music, and his mother, Ya-Wen Lo, was an opera singer. Hiao-Tsiun was born in Shanghai, in China, and Ya-Wen was born in Hong Kong. They met at a university in Chongqing, where Hiao-Tsiun was teaching, and Ya-Wen was studying. When Hiao-Tsiun moved to Paris, Ya-Wen followed. In 1949, they were married and Ya-Wen changed her name to Marina Ma.

They had two children: a girl named Yeou-Cheng, born in 1951, and four years later, on October 7, 1955, a baby boy. They decided to name him Yo, which meant "friend." But Yo Ma didn't sound quite right to his parents' ears; they wanted a more musical-sounding name, a name that flowed. So, they added a second Yo, giving their son the name Yo-Yo Ma.

Yo-Yo's father was a graduate student at the Paris Conservatory of Music, and the family lived in a one-room apartment that was partially paid for by the university. The apartment had no heat, and the first winter of Yo-Yo's life was a bitterly cold one. Even indoors, the temperature was freezing. Yo-Yo's father taught extra students to cover the cost of a hotel room for his wife and baby. He thought the hotel would be warmer than the apartment, where he stayed with Yeou-Cheng. Unfortunately, the hotel manager turned the heat off at night to save money, and the room would grow so cold that Marina feared her baby might freeze to death.

But Yo-Yo survived that cold winter, and finally spring arrived. A larger apartment became available in their building, and the family moved. Now they had two rooms: Marina and the kids slept in one, and Hiao-Tsiun slept, played music, and studied in the other.

While Hiao-Tsiun finished his studies, Marina cared for the kids, often taking them to play in the city's public gardens. Yeou-Cheng took piano lessons, astonishing her teacher with her talent. Yo-Yo also seemed to be showing musical ability: even as a toddler, he could sing perfectly in tune. He had a remarkable memory, too—although his father didn't seem to recognize this at first. One day, when Yo-Yo was jumping around singing a song about a frog, he repeated the last line instead of ending the song. Hearing this, his father said Yo-Yo would never amount to much. "Our son is a little good for nothing," he complained. "Yo-Yo has such a poor memory." Yo-Yo's mother laughed. "He's only two years old!" she reminded him.

When Yo-Yo was three, his parents decided it was time for him to join his sister in taking piano lessons. His teacher was impressed with his ability, and one day when his parents came to pick him up from his lesson, she urged him to show them what he could do. But he refused. His father, embarrassed, told him to obey his teacher. Still, Yo-Yo wouldn't play. But his mom understood: Yo-Yo was a perfectionist. He would not play for anyone else until he was happy with his performance.

Yo-Yo also tried playing the violin, but he wasn't enthusiastic about it. "I don't like the sound violins make," he told his father. "I want a big instrument." When he attended a concert with his father, he saw the one he wanted: the largest instrument in the string section of the orchestra, a huge double bass. His father tried to talk him out of it, telling him it was far too big for a three-year-old. He thought his son would forget about it, but Yo-Yo kept asking. When his father finally brought home a cello, Yo-Yo was thrilled. It wasn't as big as the double bass, but it was much bigger than the violin. Later, Yo-Yo told his mom the real reason he hadn't wanted to play the violin was that his older sister was better at it than he was.

Yo-Yo's father was determined to raise his son to be a musician, and he began teaching Yo-Yo himself. Hiao-Tsiun was strict and expected his son to work hard. Sometimes Yo-Yo found ways to rebel without directly disobeying his father's rules. When his father forbade him from going into the studio while Yeou-Cheng practiced, Yo-Yo stood in the open doorway and shot spitballs at his sister!

When Yo-Yo was playing his cello, nothing distracted him, but when his lessons finished, he changed completely—sometimes he would jump up and start leaping around the room! He was a very curious kid, and his mom always answered his questions as if he was a much older child. At bedtime, she would lie down in her bed as the kids climbed into their bunk bed, and they would talk. She would ask them about their day, and she would share advice, encouraging them to always have a positive outlook on life.

Yo-Yo was just five years old when he played his first concert, at the University of Paris. He played both cello and piano and performed pieces by Bach—it was difficult and complex music, and learning it was an astonishing feat for such a young child.

In 1962, the Ma family visited the United States. They spent time with Yo-Yo's uncle who lived in New York City and traveled across the country to visit Marina's sister in California. The recitals Yo-Yo and his sister gave during their stay led to an unexpected turn of events: Hiao-Tsiun was invited to establish a children's orchestra—his lifelong dream—and the family's visit to New York became a permanent move.

In November of that year, Yo-Yo played at a
fundraiser concert in Washington, DC. President John
F. Kennedy and First Lady Jacqueline Kennedy were in
the audience, along with former President Dwight
Eisenhower. The *New York Times* published a story
about the event; it was the first time Yo-Yo's name
appeared in a major newspaper.

Yo-Yo worked very hard to improve his skill on the
cello. There were times when he didn't feel like
practicing, but he never wanted to quit. "My love of
music kept me going," he said.

When Yo-Yo was nine, he began studying with a
new teacher, Leonard Rose. The first time Yo-Yo played
for him was at a studio in the apartment Leonard

shared with his family. Leonard could hardly believe his ears; he burst out of the studio and told his wife and daughter, who'd been listening from the kitchen, that Yo-Yo was the most talented student he'd ever heard.

At first, Yo-Yo was intimidated by his new teacher. He recalled, "I was a pipsqueak of a kid, and overwhelmingly shy. I was afraid to speak to Mr. Rose above a whisper. . . . I'd try to hide behind the cello." But Mr. Rose was kind and encouraging, explaining that he had also been shy. "He tried to get me to overcome my timidity," Yo-Yo said. "I was amazed to hear phrases coming from a fifty-year-old man such as 'Sock it to me, baby!'"

By the time Yo-Yo was in fifth grade, he felt like he was living in two different worlds. At school, he was

encouraged to think for himself. At home, he was
expected to never question his parents. "My home life
was totally structured," he explained. "Because I
couldn't rebel there, I did so at school." Yo-Yo began
skipping classes and spent a lot of time wandering
through the streets, just wanting to be alone.

Despite his frequent absences, Yo-Yo graduated from
high school when he was just fifteen. That summer, he
went to a music camp called Meadowmount. Yo-Yo had
never stayed away from home before! Overwhelmed by
his sudden independence, he skipped rehearsals, left his
cello outdoors where it could have been damaged by
rain, and got in trouble for writing graffiti on a wall.
"Suddenly, I was free," he said. "I had always kept my
emotions bottled up, but at Meadowmount I just ran
wild."

When camp ended, Yo-Yo faced a difficult decision: should he work at his music career full-time or pursue further education? He loved music, but he also loved to learn—so he decided to do both.

For the next four years, Yo-Yo studied at Harvard University, in Massachusetts. He took courses in history, anthropology, art, literature, math, sociology, and science, but he played so many concerts that it was hard to find time to study! "I even thought of leaving school, but my father insisted that I stay, and limit my concerts to one a month," he said. Yo-Yo was glad he followed that advice; he found that his studies helped him to better understand the history and diversity of the world around him. At nineteen, he also began studying at Juilliard, where his teacher and mentor Leonard Rose was an instructor.

Today, Yo-Yo has recorded more than one hundred albums, won nineteen Grammy awards, and toured the world, performing as a soloist with orchestras in many countries. He is best known for his classical music, but he has also recorded American bluegrass music, traditional Chinese music, Argentinian tangos, and music from Brazil! He's collaborated with many other musicians, including Miley Cyrus, Bobby McFerrin, and James Taylor. In 2021, Yo-Yo Ma's performance of "Amazing Grace" was played during the inauguration of US president Joe Biden.

Yo-Yo also founded a not-for-profit organization called Silk Road, which connects musicians, composers, and audiences around the world and fosters international understanding through music. In 2006, he became the tenth person appointed to the United Nations Messengers of Peace—a small group of dedicated public figures who work to raise awareness of the UN and its efforts to improve the lives of billions of people around the world. Singer-songwriter Stevie Wonder, Chinese pianist Lang Lang, and Japanese American violinist Midori Goto are also UN Messengers for Peace.

The 1920s, also known as the Roaring Twenties, was a time of excitement and change. World War I was over, the economy was booming, and hope was in the air. America's cities were alive with musical creativity, and despite a ban on alcohol sales, night clubs and dance bands flourished. Jazz and blues music, which had roots deeply intertwined with the Black American experience, led to great creative expression and innovation, and served as a catalyst for social change.

Known as the Jazz Age, this decade saw some of the greatest musicians of all time step into the spotlight. In New Orleans, Jelly Roll Morton became the first jazz musician to write down his musical arrangements. Louis Armstrong, Duke Ellington, and King Oliver became stars in New Orleans, New York, and Chicago. Blues singers Ma Rainey—who mesmerized audiences with her showy outfits, ostrich feathers, and gold teeth—and Bessie Smith became icons of the era. The legacy and influence of the Jazz Age continues today.

THREE

SONGWRITING AND MUSIC-MAKING

WEAVING STORIES INTO SONGS,

★ ★ ★ these ★ ★ ★

TALENTED

YOUNG ARTISTS

★ ★ ★ wrote ★ ★ ★

LYRICS AND MELODIES

THAT LEFT

THEIR MARK

★ ON MUSIC ★

HISTORY.

Paul McCartney

A Far-off Dream

Paul McCartney is a singer, a songwriter, and a bass player—and most famously, he was a member of the iconic 1960s band the Beatles. As a teenager making music with his friends, Paul had no idea that his childhood home would one day be a tourist attraction.

Paul was born on June 18, 1942, in Liverpool, England. His father, Jim, missed his birth; Paul was born in the middle of World War II, when England was being bombed by Germany, and Jim was working as a volunteer firefighter. He remembered arriving at the hospital to join his wife, Mary, and meet their new son: "He had one eye open and he squawked all the time," Jim said. They named the baby James Paul McCartney, but they always called him Paul.

Paul's little brother, Mike, arrived less than two years later, and a year after that, the war finally ended. Across the country, people celebrated with bonfires and fireworks. Jim went back to his previous job as a cotton salesman, and Mary found a job as a midwife. One of Paul's earliest memories was of Mary heading out on her bicycle to help deliver a baby in the middle of the night, the streets covered in snow.

Liverpool was badly damaged by wartime bombing, and Paul and his brother often played in the demolished buildings and craters, which they referred to as "bombies." The British economy was also in bad shape, but Paul's family had enough money to live comfortably. His family took vacations in the summers, often going to seaside towns where they could play on the beach.

Paul enjoyed school. He was left-handed—but luckily, his teachers accepted this and did not try to force him to use his right hand, as many teachers did in those days. He particularly enjoyed writing, and when he was ten, he won a prize for an essay about the upcoming coronation of Queen Elizabeth II. It was a topic everyone was talking about: a new monarch, after the death of England's king in 1952. Paul's parents bought their first television, a small black-and-white one, and friends and relatives crowded into their living room to watch the crowning of the young queen.

At age twelve, Paul started attending the Liverpool Institute High School for Boys, where he earned the nickname Macca—a shortened version of McCartney. He found schoolwork easy but sometimes got in trouble for talking in class. The school had an outstanding music teacher, but Paul didn't take advantage of this; he wanted to do things in his own way and didn't like being told what to do. This was true at home as well. His father, who had once led a jazz band, wanted Paul to take piano lessons, but Paul preferred teaching himself on the family's piano.

In 1955, the family moved to a new home at 20 Forthlin Road. They had a telephone installed so Mary could be reached when her help was needed to deliver a baby. It was the only phone on the street, so neighbors often came over to make calls. Behind the house was a police training school, and Paul and his brother, Mike, put chairs on the garden shed roof so they could watch the officers train their dogs and exercise their horses.

When Paul was fourteen, his mom was diagnosed with breast cancer. In those days, treatments for cancer were not as advanced as they are today, and she died a few months later. Paul and Mike hadn't been told that she was ill, and her death came as a terrible shock. The whole family was devastated, but Paul tried to keep his painful emotions hidden away. "I learned to put a shell around me," he said.

Paul's aunts and uncles pitched in to help the family, visiting often and cooking them many dinners. Music was also a source of comfort: American rock and roll was finally reaching the UK, and Paul was obsessed with Elvis Presley, the young American star who was being hailed as the King of Rock and Roll. He even copied Elvis's hairstyle and tight-fitting pants! Most adults didn't approve of Elvis, and his music wasn't played on the radio as much as Paul would've liked. Luckily, some stores had special cubicles where people could listen to their favorite songs for free: "To hear 'Heartbreak Hotel' I had to go into a record shop in Liverpool and listen to it through headphones in one of those booths," Paul recalled. Paul also discovered Little Richard, and used to practice the singer's famous scream!

Paul's dad had given him a trumpet for his thirteenth birthday, but Paul was more interested in rock and roll, so he traded in his trumpet for a guitar. His best friend, Ian James, taught him some basic chords, but Paul found playing awkward and frustrating. One day, he saw a left-handed guitarist on a concert poster, and he realized why he was having trouble! He switched his guitar around, strumming with his left hand instead of his right.

When Paul was fifteen, he went to an outdoor event to see a local band called the Quarrymen. The Quarrymen was a skiffle band, playing on homemade instruments: cheap guitars, washboards scraped with thimbles, and a wooden tea chest with a broom handle. Skiffle bands had been popular in the US in the 1920s, and in the mid-1950s, they made a comeback in England.

A boy named John Lennon was the Quarrymen's leader. He was a neighbor of Paul's, and nearly two years older. After the show, Paul hung out with the band, picking up one of their guitars and singing. A few weeks later, they invited Paul to join the band. Paul's first public appearance with the Quarrymen was not a success—he was so nervous that he messed up his part quite badly—but when the group returned to the venue a month later, he performed better. A few months later, Paul's friend George Harrison, who rode the bus to school with him every day, joined the band as well.

Paul and John began writing songs together, filling a notebook with their lyrics, and by the time Paul was sixteen, he was skipping school for living-room practice sessions. When it came time to take his exams, he failed nearly all of them and had to repeat the school year.

Paul wasn't sure what he wanted to do. He had an inspiring English teacher who got him excited about literature, and his teachers encouraged him to consider a career in teaching, but Paul was dreaming about music. "It was," he admitted, "a bit of a far-off dream."

It didn't help that things weren't going well with the band. Their drummer had quit, and without a drummer, no one would hire them. Eight months went by, and their only opportunity to play had been at a party held by Paul's aunt! But by 1960, the group had found a drummer, changed their name to the Beatles, and—just two months after Paul turned eighteen—headed off to Germany to play a series of shows.

Paul had no way of knowing that he was embarking on a path that would change the world of music forever. In 1962, the Beatles released their first single, "Love Me Do"—one of the first songs Paul and John wrote together. By this time, Paul was playing bass. Ringo Starr had become the band's drummer, joining Paul, John, and George to make up what would soon be known as the Fab Four.

Over the next two years the Beatles released hit after hit, touring the world and becoming so popular that huge crowds of wildly enthusiastic fans greeted them everywhere they went. Newspapers even invented a word to describe the frenzy of excitement: Beatlemania!

The Beatles became one of the most influential
bands of all time, and Paul and John cowrote hundreds
of songs, many of which are still played today.
"Yesterday," which was written mainly by Paul, has
been performed and recorded by so many musicians—
from Elvis Presley and Marvin Gaye to the Royal
Philharmonic Orchestra—that it set a Guinness World
Record! After the Beatles stopped playing together,
Paul formed the band Wings, which became one of the
most popular bands of the 1970s, releasing hits such as
"Band on the Run," "Silly Love Songs," and "Mull of
Kintyre." After Wings disbanded, Paul continued to
write and perform as a solo artist.

In 1979, Paul McCartney was awarded the Guinness
World Record for the most successful songwriter in
music history. He has been awarded a knighthood for

his services to music, giving him the title of Sir James Paul McCartney. In 2023, more than sixty years after his first hit, Paul McCartney was still making music and performing live around the world! He has also used his fame to work for causes that are important to him, such as animal rights and the environment.

Joni Mitchell

Painting with Words

Blending jazz, rock, and folk, Joni Mitchell's songs captured the spirit of her generation and made her an icon during the 1960s and 1970s. Today, she is considered one of the greatest singer-songwriters of all time—but as a child, her plan was to be a painter.

Joni Mitchell was born in the Canadian prairies, in Fort Macleod, Alberta, on November 7, 1943, during the Second World War. Her father, William Andrew Anderson, was in the air force, and her mother, Myrtle Marguerite McKee, was a schoolteacher. Joni's full name was Roberta Joan Anderson, but everyone called her Joan.

After the war, the family moved from Alberta to Saskatchewan. They settled in the town of North Battleford, where Joan's father ran the local grocery store. Joan and her friend Marilyn used to spend hours looking at the Simpson-Sears catalog together and picking out their favorite things—from clothes to hammers and saws! The catalog seemed incredibly glamorous to them, so they called it the Book of Dreams.

Growing up on the prairies meant cold winters, wide open spaces, and big blue skies. "I lived in the tail end of a horse drawn culture," Joni said. "We still had our water and the milk delivered by horses." Her mom, Myrtle, reinforced Joni's love of nature, taking her out to the fields and teaching her bird calls.

When Joan was in third grade, she had an experience that made her dislike school: Her teacher gave the class a test and then sorted them by how well they did. The students who got A's were called the Bluebirds, the B students were the Robins, the C students were the Wrens, and the students who scored lowest were the Crows. To Joan, sitting in the row with the Wrens, it all seemed wrong; she remembered thinking that the A and B kids weren't actually smarter, just better at repeating what the teacher wanted them to say.

North Battleford hosted an annual music competition and Joan always attended. "You could go to the church and listen to the choirs compete or you could go to school," she explained. "I went to the church." Joan didn't enter the competition, but several of her friends did, including her close friend Frankie, a talented piano player.

Frankie's father was the school principal and to the horror of Joan's mother, Myrtle, he sometimes allowed Frankie and Joan to skip school to go to the movies. One of the movies they saw had a piece of classical music by the Russian composer Sergei Rachmaninoff as its theme song, and Joan couldn't stop thinking about it. "That piece of music thrilled me to no end," she said. "It was the most beautiful piece of music that I ever heard."

Joan desperately wanted the Rachmaninoff record, but her parents said it was too expensive. In those days, many stores had listening booths where you could play records without purchasing them, so Joan started going to Grubman's department store two or three times a week to listen to it. It was this piece of music, she said later, that made her want to be a musician.

A few days after Joan's tenth birthday, she felt so tired and achy that she had to sit down and rest on her way to school. The next day, when she couldn't get out of bed, she was diagnosed with polio.

Today, polio is prevented through vaccination—but in 1953, a vaccine for polio wasn't yet available. The polio virus could cause paralysis and, in the worst cases, could affect the muscles needed to breathe. Thousands of patients, many of them children, had to spend weeks or months in special breathing machines called iron lungs. Between the 1920s and the 1950s, polio epidemics hit parts of Canada and the US in one wave after another.

Public health officials gave daily updates; schools, playgrounds, and movie theaters were closed; and people who were infected were placed in quarantine. For Joan, that meant being sent to a special polio hospital in Saskatoon. She found it frightening to be away from her family, and she hated listening to the wheezing sound of the iron lungs all night long. What if she needed to go in one of those machines? What if she could never walk again?

To Joan's distress, she had to stay in the hospital over Christmas. Myrtle visited, bringing a small Christmas tree. As Joan recovered she needed physical therapy to learn to walk again, but at last she was well enough to go home.

The following year, when Joan was eleven, her family moved to Saskatoon and she began attending Queen Elizabeth School. At this new school, she met someone who would become an important part of her journey toward becoming a songwriter: her seventh-grade teacher, Arthur Kratzmann. He seemed to share her rebellious spirit; she remembered him coming into the classroom and announcing that he didn't think much of the curriculum! Joan loved art and painting, so Mr. Kratzmann told her, "If you can paint with a brush, you can paint with words." Years later, she dedicated her first album to him, saying that he taught her to love words.

But for the most part, Joan found school frustrating and wanted to spend all her time on art. "I would line the math room with ink drawings and portraits of the mathematicians," she said. One of her art teachers was named Henry Bonli, and Joan liked the look of the *-i* ending of his signature—so, at fourteen, she changed her name to Joni.

As a teenager, Joni had a lot of conflict with her mother. Sometimes Myrtle would say, "Don't have kids when you get grown," which Joni found terribly insulting. Was her mom suggesting that Joni was a nuisance? Joni was artistic and strong-willed, and she struggled to understand her more conservative mother. Their house illustrated the differences between them: it was spotlessly clean and decorated in neutral colors—except Joni's room, where Joni had painted a tree on her wall!

Joni loved music and dancing. She was a fan of artists such as Chuck Berry, Ray Charles, and Elvis Presley, and she went dancing with a friend several times a week at the YMCA—in fact, she organized Wednesday night dances because it was too hard to wait for the weekend! She went to parties and wiener roasts by the riverbank and hung around downtown

Saskatoon with friends. Her mother worried about her daughter getting into trouble—and sometimes Joni gave Myrtle reason to worry. In eleventh grade, Joni was driven home by the police when she was caught shoplifting a pair of pants. Joni's mom paid for the pants and Joni never did anything like that again—but she felt that Myrtle never forgave or trusted her after that.

At parties and bonfires, Joni and her friends enjoyed singing together, and Joni thought it would be fun to get a guitar so she could play along. Her mom wouldn't help her buy one—Myrtle thought Joni wouldn't stick with it—so Joni saved up enough to buy a cheaper ukulele instead. Polio had left some of the muscles in her hands weak, so as she taught herself to play, she also had to find different techniques that worked for her.

Joni's plan was to go art school and be a painter—but somehow, she just couldn't put that ukelele down. Her first paid performance was at a Saskatoon folk and jazz club, just before her nineteenth birthday. Joni managed to graduate from high school—despite failing math and chemistry and physics and having to take the courses a second time—and she moved to Calgary to study at the Alberta College of Art. While she was a student there, she got a guitar and began teaching herself to play and sing. By the time she was twenty, she'd dropped out of art school and started playing three nights a week at a Calgary night club.

In 1964, Joni moved to Toronto. She was broke, with just sixty dollars in her pocket, and she was pregnant. Joni found work at clubs, playing on the local folk music scene to pay the rent—but she knew she couldn't do that once she had a baby to look after. So Joni made the difficult decision to place her daughter for adoption and in 1965, aged twenty-two, she moved to the United States to pursue her career as a folk singer.

Joni quickly became a hit in Detroit, which led to opportunities to perform in New York and around the country. She began gaining success first as a songwriter, writing songs for singers like Buffy Sainte-Marie and Judy Collins. Some of her songs, such as "The Circle Game," "Both Sides, Now," and "Chelsea

Morning," became hits. In 1968, she released her first album of songs that she wrote and played by herself.

Over the next four decades, Joni Mitchell went on to win ten Grammy Awards, including a lifetime achievement award. From her unconventional guitar playing and deeply personal song lyrics, to producing many of her own albums and designing their covers, she has always been determined to do things her own way. In 2023, at nearly eighty years old, Joni delighted her fans with a triumphant return to the stage at her first scheduled concert in more than two decades.

Bob Marley

A Message of Love

Jamaican singer-songwriter Bob Marley is a
world-renowned reggae musician and one
of the most influential musicians of the twentieth
century. His music and lyrics reflect his love for
his country, as well as the poverty and racism he
experienced growing up.

Bob Marley was born on February 6, 1945, in a tiny village in St. Ann Parish, Jamaica. The village was named Nine Mile because it was nine miles from the nearest town. His mother's name was Cedella Malcom, but most people knew her as Ciddy. She was eighteen years old when she married Bob's father, Norval Sinclair Marley.

In those days, Jamaica was a colony under British rule—and it had been for almost three hundred years. Norval worked for the British government, overseeing property in the village. His and Ciddy's marriage was considered shocking by many in the community: Norval was over sixty years old when they wed, and while Ciddy was Black, he was white. During the 1940s in Jamaica, interracial marriage was neither common nor widely accepted.

Not long after the wedding, their baby was born in Ciddy's father's farmhouse. Norval—who was often called by his nickname, Captain—was away at the time of the birth, but he returned a few days later and named the boy Nesta Robert Marley. Ciddy wasn't sure what to make of the name Nesta: it sounded too much like Lester and she thought that would confuse people. Norval didn't explain his reason for the name, but Ciddy later discovered that Nesta meant messenger. The middle name, Robert, was in honor of Norval's brother, who had been a well-known cricket and tennis player.

Norval left the family soon after Nesta's birth, and Ciddy raised her son in a one-room house on a hill, surrounded by fruit trees of all kinds: mango, banana, and coconut; orange and grapefruit; jackfruit and star apple. There was no electricity or running water in the village, so the house had a pile of stones outside that was used as a stove, and the toilet was an outhouse. When it rained, Nesta helped collect rainwater for drinking, cooking, and washing. Nine Mile was a beautiful place and Nesta loved it. He used to wake up early and explore the forested areas nearby or lay on a big rock staring up at the sky.

When Nesta was four years old, he began going to nearby Stepney School. He learned quickly—in fact, he often helped the other kids with their reading and math. At lunch, he played soccer, using an orange or a grapefruit as a ball. But what he liked best of all was singing, often very quietly. When a local singing contest was held, Nesta entered—and won a pound!

Nesta and Ciddy's house belonged to Ciddy's father, Omeriah Malcolm. He also owned thirty acres of land on a nearby mountaintop. When he wasn't at school, young Nesta would wake up before the sun and walk through the hills to his grandfather's property to work. Once there, he often rode his grandfather's gray horse or a donkey named Nimble.

Nesta and his cousins Sledger and Lloyd planted crops such as cocoa beans, corn, and sugarcane. They prepared the fields for growing yams: clearing the ground, digging holes, and planting cuttings from old yams in each hole.

When the work was done, Nesta would sometimes gallop away on the big gray horse, down the hills to his grandfather's house, and jump right over the five-foot-high gate! His cousin Sledger said that Nesta stuck to the horse's back as tightly as a tick.

Nesta's grandfather had an organ, a banjo, and a fiddle. He also owned one of the few electrical generators in the area, and he used it to power his radio. On Sundays, his family, friends, and neighbors would gather around to listen as he played music from radio stations in Miami or Cuba. Nesta liked dance music best—he was a fan of Elvis Presley and Fats Domino. Nesta also heard a lot of music in church, and years later he spoke of how that influenced him: "We used to go to church and hear plenty singing, and watch people get in the spirit," he said.

When Nesta was five or six, his mother received a letter from his father asking her to send Nesta to the capital city of Kingston for tutoring. Kingston was a three-hour drive away, but Ciddy agreed and Norval came to pick him up. Instead of keeping Nesta with him in Kingston, though, Norval brought him to the home of an elderly white woman named Mrs. Grey. More than a year went by, and Ciddy didn't know where her son was or when she would see him again. Luckily, a friend of hers spotted Nesta out walking in the city one day—and Ciddy traveled to Kingston to bring her son back home to Nine Mile.

Back at the Stepney School, Nesta found a best friend. His name was Neville O'Riley Livingston, but everyone called him Bunny. Bunny had just spent a year in Kingston, and he had brought something wonderful back with him: a guitar! It was homemade, constructed from bamboo, electrical wire, and a sardine can. Nesta was fascinated by the music Bunny played on it—songs he had heard on the radio in Kingston. He wanted to learn to play guitar and write songs of his own.

When Nesta was twelve, his mother and Bunny's father, Thaddius Livingston, began a relationship, and the four of them—Ciddy and Thaddius, Nesta and Bunny—all moved to Kingston together. Bunny said that he and Nesta were like brothers. "We grew up as family," he explained.

They settled in a neighborhood known as Trench Town. There, Nesta began going by his middle name, Robert, and then Bob: a new name for a new phase of his life. Life in the city wasn't easy at first. Bob's family didn't have much money, and Trench Town was crowded and rundown. Bob was bullied, partly because of his light skin, and got into a lot of fights. "Why is my father white and not black like everybody else? What did I do wrong?" he asked his mother. He was angry that his father had abandoned the family, too.

Living under the same roof in Trench Town, Bob and Bunny grew closer and their friendship became stronger than ever. Their parents had a baby together, so they now shared a younger sister: Claudette Pearl. They both loved cricket and soccer, and—most of all—

music. Now that he was a teenager, Bob was becoming more serious about singing and songwriting, but his mother thought he should do something more practical. Reluctantly, Bob took a job as a welder. He hated it, and one day while he was working a shard of metal flew into his face, injuring his eye. That was the end of his welding career.

When Bob was seventeen, his mother moved to the United States and remarried. Bob decided to stay in Kingston. He recorded his first songs that year, but they weren't successful. He decided that being a solo artist wasn't for him—he had more fun singing with friends—so he, Bunny, and four other teenagers formed a vocal group. They thought about calling themselves the Teenagers, or the Roosters—but eventually they became the Wailers.

These were hard times for Bob. He didn't have much money and often didn't have enough to eat. By the time the Wailers recorded their first single, Bob was homeless and sleeping on the floor in a back room at the recording studio. That single was Bob's song "Simmer Down." Rather than imitating popular songs from America, it spoke directly to the people he'd grown up with in Kingston's Trench Town neighborhood—and by February 1964, when Bob turned nineteen, it was the number one hit in Jamaica. The group released their first album the following year. It was called *The Wailing Wailers*, and it included the now-famous song "One Love." The song catapulted the Wailers to worldwide recognition. Bob Marley went on to release many renowned songs, both with the band and later as a solo artist.

Sadly, Bob Marley died in 1981, at just thirty-six years of age—but his music lived on, and his songs like "Redemption Song" and "Get Up, Stand Up" have become important symbols of freedom and resistance for many people around the world. His greatest hits album, *Legend*, became the best-selling reggae album in history. Bob Marley has also been honored with a Grammy Lifetime Achievement Award and a star on the Hollywood Walk of Fame—but fame was never his goal. He wanted to change the world for the better, and he wrote songs that showed his passion for music and his love for people—especially those who are oppressed and facing hardship or injustice.

Dolly Parton

Born Restless

With a career spanning five decades, Dolly Parton is a country music legend. Her songwriting skills, voice, and style made her famous, but she is also loved for her down-to-earth warmth, quick wit, and generous spirit. As a small child, she sang to an audience of chickens, ducks, and pigs!

Dolly Rebecca Parton was born on January 19, 1946, in a one-room cabin in the foothills of East Tennessee's Great Smoky Mountains. Her parents, Avie Lee Parton and Robert Lee Parton, didn't have money to pay the doctor who delivered the baby, so they gave him a sack of cornmeal instead.

Dolly was the fourth of their children, and over the next few years, she was followed by eight more. Avie and Robert were sharecroppers, living and farming on land that belonged to an old woman who lived near the family's cabin. Dolly knew her as Aunt Marth, and was often left with her as a toddler. Aunt Marth used to sing a song as she bounced Dolly on her knee: it began, "Tiptoe, tiptoe, little Dolly Parton." Dolly was amazed that there was a song with her name in it and she begged Aunt Marth to sing it again and again. "It never occurred to me you could put anybody's name in the song," she said.

When Dolly was five, her family moved to a new home, a farm in nearby Locust Ridge, near Sevierville. It had just one bedroom and the roof leaked, but it was their own. The walls of the house were covered with newspaper to seal the cracks. Dolly liked to read the newspaper, especially the comic strips—although, she said, "sometimes you'd have to stand on your head to read something that had been pasted on upside down."

Dolly's family had lots of animals on their farm—but the kids badly wanted a pony. "We used to dream about having a pony and how wonderful he would be," Dolly said. Their Uncle Dot had a solution: they could grow one, he told them. They begged to know how. "By planting pony seeds, of course!" he told them. Pony seeds, the kids concluded, must come from horses. "We studied turds for hours," Dolly said. "We planted our horse turds and weeded them and watered them." She truly believed that one day they would find a row of ponies growing in the yard.

Dolly's family couldn't afford store-bought toys but her dad whittled toys out of wood, and her mom made her a doll from a corn cob, with corn silk for hair and a dress made of corn husks. This doll inspired Dolly's first song! Dolly sang, "Little Tiny Tasseltop, you're the only friend I got . . ." and her mom wrote down the words. Even as a five-year-old, she had a knack for rhyme. Dolly didn't always have the audience she dreamed of, but that didn't stop her. If her siblings weren't available to listen, she'd even sing to the family's chickens!

That same year, Dolly started kindergarten in a one-room schoolhouse. She didn't like school, but she loved to learn and she read everything she could get her hands on. When she read a book about China, she was fascinated. She wanted to go to this country on the other side of the world. Dolly convinced the other kids to help her dig, and they secretly worked at it for months. "I was just convinced we were going to break through to China any minute," Dolly said.

Dolly enjoyed making up stories of her own even more than reading. When she had to do book reports for school, she sometimes made up a title, author, and story and gave her report on the book she had invented!

Makeup fascinated Dolly, too, and she made her own. The orangey-red medicine her mom painted on her kids' cuts and scrapes worked as lipstick, flour became face powder, and the blackened end of a burned match served as eyeliner, especially if Dolly licked it to make it wet. She burned her tongue a few times because she was too impatient to wait for the match to cool down!

Her mom understood Dolly's desire to stand out, so she collected scraps of cloth and made Dolly a special coat. Dolly put it on proudly. "I burst through the school doors like a multicolored whirlwind," she said. The other kids laughed at her. "It looks like a bunch of rags," one boy said. Dolly was heartbroken, but she refused to take the coat off. Years later, she wrote a song about it. "Coat of Many Colors" was a huge hit and Dolly's favorite of all the songs she wrote.

Despite her loving family, Dolly often felt lonely and impatient. "I was born restless," she said. "I was just different, and I knew it." She wanted to see the world, and she had big dreams about her future as a singer. She'd been singing in local churches with her sisters since she was six, and she loved writing songs. Anything that had a rhythm—her mom snapping beans, the wild geese honking—could start a song for her. She'd snap her fingers or bang a spoon on a pot, making up the words to sing along. She played a homemade guitar—a mandolin with guitar strings—

until she was eight, when one of her uncles got her a real guitar. "I would sit up on top of the woodpile playing and singing at the top of my lungs," she said. Sometimes she'd pretend her porch was a stage and use a tobacco stake with a tin can on top as a microphone. But she wanted a bigger audience—one that wasn't made of chicken and ducks and her younger siblings.

When Dolly was ten, her Uncle Bill introduced her to Cas Walker, a local businessman and celebrity. Cas gave her a chance to sing on his radio and television shows. Dolly loved it, and soon she was earning five dollars for each appearance. Once, Cas offered $250 to anyone who could climb a greasy pole—polished wood slicked with lard—and Dolly decided to give it a try. She was a good climber, but more importantly, she had a clever plan: she rolled around in the dirt parking lot first, figuring that the mud and sand would help her grip the slippery pole. Sure enough, it worked! Dolly used the money to buy a television for her family.

Unfortunately, some of Dolly's classmates were jealous of her local fame, and one day at school a group of them locked her in the cloakroom. It was dark, and she was scared. She banged on the door, but they left her in there for what felt to Dolly like a very long time. This experience left Dolly with a lifelong fear of the dark.

But nothing could put a dent in her dreams of being a star. Dolly recorded her first song, "Puppy Love," when she was twelve, and she spent vacations with her relatives in Knoxville, where she could do television and radio shows. Her Uncle Bill took her on trips to Nashville, driving old, beat-up cars that they'd sleep in at night, and he talked to everyone they met about his talented niece. His plan worked: at age thirteen, Dolly gave her first performance at the Grand Ole Opry, where she was introduced by the famous country singer-songwriter Johnny Cash. The audience loved her, and she got three encores! Walking back to the car afterward, she turned to her uncle and said, "I'm pretty good, ain't I?"

My friend, Miss Dolly!

But Dolly still had to get through high school, where she was badly bullied. Luckily, she had a good friend named Judy. The two girls joined the high school band and spent many hours together in the band room, with Dolly making up songs on the piano and Judy writing them down. Dolly said they were as close as sisters.

Finally, graduation day arrived. The students stood up, one at a time, to announce their plans for the future. When it was Dolly's turn, she shared her own: "I'm going to Nashville to become a star." Everyone started laughing! This just made Dolly even more determined to succeed. The next morning, she boarded a Greyhound bus, and with her old guitar and her songs, she was on her way to Nashville.

Breaking into the music industry was tough, and sometimes Dolly was so poor she couldn't afford to eat. But she was unstoppable, and when she was twenty-one, her first album was released. It was called *Hello, I'm Dolly*.

Dolly Parton went on to release many more albums, selling more than 100 million records worldwide. She has written many famous songs, including "I Will Always Love You" and "Jolene." In 1980, she agreed to play a leading role in the movie *Nine to Five*—on the condition that she could also write its theme song! Dolly was a natural actress and the movie was a hit, propelling Dolly's fame to new heights. In 1999 she was inducted into the Country Music Hall of Fame, and in 2022 she was inducted into the Rock and Roll Hall of Fame.

Today, Dolly is loved not just for her music but also for her kindness and generosity. She has used her success to support education and literacy, especially for children growing up in poverty. In 1995, she started

Dolly Parton's Imagination Library to help get books into the hands of young readers—and by 2023, the program was sending more than two million free books to children every month.

Throughout history, music has been linked with social change. During the civil rights movement, Nina Simone released her first protest song, "Mississippi Goddam" —it was her response to several recent acts of racist violence. Nina believed that an artist's duty was to reflect the times they lived in.

When young Americans organized to protest the Vietnam War, musicians joined them. Singer-songwriter Phil Ochs wrote many anti-war songs, including "The War Is Over," which he performed live for 150,000 anti-war demonstrators. Former Beatles singer John Lennon released "Give Peace a Chance." Marvin Gaye, Pete Seeger, Bob Dylan, Neil Young, Joni Mitchell, and many others released songs that became part of the soundtrack of the anti-war movement of the 1960s and '70s.

Today, musicians continue to reflect the world around them, writing songs that protest police violence, racism, poverty, and injustice and using music to bring about a better world.

FOUR

RHYTHM AND BLUES AND THE MOTOWN SOUND

THESE
MUSICAL LEGENDS
★ ★ BROKE NEW GROUND, ★ ★
MAKING HISTORY
AND BREAKING
RACIAL BARRIERS
★ ★ ★ AS THEY BROUGHT ★ ★ ★
YOUNG PEOPLE
TOGETHER
TO DANCE TO THEIR
★ ★ ★ SOULFUL ★ ★ ★
MELODIES.

Diana Ross

Hitsville USA

From "Stop! In the Name of Love" to "I Will Survive," Diana Ross's singing has been heard around the world for over half a century. In kindergarten, she liked organizing her classmates to put on shows—and she always made sure that she had the starring role.

Diana Ross's parents, Fred and Ernestine, met in Detroit and married in 1941. Diana, born on March 26, 1944, was their second child. Her parents had intended to name her Diane, but a clerk's error led to the name Diana appearing on her birth certificate!

Diana was born during the Second World War, and when she was three months old, Fred was drafted into the military and sent to the Philippines. With Fred away, money was tight, so Ernestine did various jobs: teaching basketball, running sewing classes, and working as a kindergarten teacher.

Finally, the war ended and Fred came home. Detroit's automotive industry was booming; in fact, Detroit's nickname was Motor City. Many Black people had moved there, looking for better jobs and fleeing the racist discrimination and violence in the South. This was part of a larger movement known as the Great Migration, which began around 1910 and saw millions of Black Americans move north.

Living in a mostly Black neighborhood meant that Diana experienced less exposure to racism in her daily life—but in the news, she saw images of police violence, mobs of white people protesting integration, and Black people being arrested for fighting for civil rights. "I knew from an early age that my journey would be harder than others . . . because black people have to strive harder," she said.

By first grade, Diana had three more siblings and the apartment was bursting at the seams. Diana was scrappy and enjoyed roughhousing. But her mom didn't approve of her scuffles with neighborhood kids: "I'm serious, Diana," Ernestine said. "No more fighting."

When Diana was seven, her mom became ill with an infectious disease called tuberculosis. In those days, people with tuberculosis were sent for a long stay in a special hospital called a sanitorium. At the time Fred was working long hours to support the family, so Ernestine's sister agreed to look after the five children in Alabama.

Life in the South came as a shock for Diana and her siblings. In the 1950s, there were laws designed to discriminate against Black people that kept Black people and white people apart. This system was known as segregation. Water fountains and restrooms were marked "white" or "colored," and movie theaters had separate entrances and seating. By the time Ernestine recovered from tuberculosis, and the kids returned to Detroit, they were far more aware of the racism in the world outside their own neighborhood.

Sometimes, that racism turned into violence—like the day Diana came home with a bruise on her face after a boy at school hit her and called her a racist slur. Diana's mom was shaken and angry. She told Diana that if anyone ever called her that again, she wanted her to fight back. Diana was confused: her mom had always told her not to fight! But Ernestine said she had changed her mind. "Don't ever let anyone make you feel bad at yourself," she said. "You fight. And you'd better win."

In 1955, Diana and her family moved to a house on
Belmont Street, in another part of Detroit, a community
of townhouses with tidy lawns and porches with flower
boxes. It was on one of those porches that Diana used to
watch a teenage boy—the fifteen-year-old uncle of her
friend Sharon—playing music with his group. His name
was William Robinson—and he would go on to become
famous as Smokey Robinson, leader of the Motown
band called the Miracles.

Diana loved music. She listened to records by blues
singers such as Etta James, and she posed in front of
the mirror as she sang along. One night, her parents
threw a party and invited Diana to entertain their
friends. She earned enough tips to buy a new pair of tap
shoes!

The arrival of another baby meant there were now six kids in the family, so on Diana's fourteenth birthday, the family moved into low-income housing at the newly built Brewster-Douglas Project. This was the largest development owned by the city of Detroit, and the family was able to get a three-bedroom apartment for a reasonable rent. It was the kind of community where people looked out for each other: the kids played together, the teenagers sang and danced and listened to the radio, and the parents socialized in the courtyard.

One afternoon, Diana was singing on her porch with friends when a young man approached her. He knew of a musical group, he said, and he thought she'd be great in it. The group was called the Primettes, and the other three girls were the same age as Diana. "We'll have to check with my mama," Diana said, "'cause what she says, goes."

Diana's mom agreed. Her dad worried it might distract Diana from going to college—but Diana and her mom were persuasive, and he finally said yes. Diana was thrilled, and she had a wonderful time at the group's first rehearsal, where she and the other girls—Mary Wilson, Florence Ballard, and Betty McGlown—learned a Ray Charles song together. It wasn't long before they were performing onstage along with a boys' group, the Primes, and making $15 per show.

By this time, Diana was attending Cass Technical High School. Some of her teachers were frustrated by her lack of interest in their classes, but when they told her to work harder, she replied that she didn't need to because she was going to be a singer! "Singing became my life," Diana recalled. "It was all that I cared about. I had a dream, and I was completely determined to make it real."

What Diana wanted was a record contract. Her old neighbor, Smokey Robinson, had one—his record had even been played on the radio. Diana talked to him, and with his help, the Primettes were given the chance to audition for the Motown Record company, at the famous Hitsville USA recording studio. They showed up in matching white skirts and bobby socks and sang "There Goes My Baby." Berry Gordy, the founder of Motown Records, looked interested, but when he found out how young the girls were, he told them to come back after they finished high school.

Diana didn't plan to wait that long. "We're coming back here every day until something happens for us," she said. And they did! "We'd pester everybody to teach us things about singing," Diana said, "and eventually, just to get us off their backs, they would."

Their plan worked: A few months later, when Berry Gordy needed someone to contribute hand claps and vocals for a solo artist, he thought of the teenage girls who'd been hanging around the studio. The recording session went well, and by the end of the year, the Primettes had a record contract and a new group name: the Supremes.

Their first single was released in 1961, just before Diana's seventeenth birthday. It wasn't a big hit—nor was their next song, or their next. By 1963, they'd released six singles and none of them had been very successful. People around the studio began referring to them as the No-Hits Supremes.

But finally, in 1964, the Supremes had their first hit with the song "Where Did Our Love Go"—and over the year that followed, they released five number one hits in a row! The group toured all over the world and became an international sensation known for their glamorous outfits as well as their music. Diana had always loved fashion and design; she had taken modeling classes and was voted the best dressed student in her high school.

In 1967, the group was renamed Diana Ross and the Supremes, highlighting Diana's role as lead singer. Three years later, Diana released her first album as a solo artist. Over the next fifty years, many of Diana's songs became hits around the world. She also ventured into acting, winning a Golden Globe Award and an Academy Award nomination for her portrayal of the singer Billie Holiday in the 1972 movie *Lady Sings the Blues.*

Today, Diana has sold more than 100 million records. She has been inducted to the Rock and Roll Hall of Fame, won a Grammy Lifetime Achievement Award, and been honored with two stars on the Hollywood Walk of Fame—one as a member of the Supremes, and one as a solo artist. In 2016, Barack Obama awarded her the Presidential Medal of Freedom. Diana Ross, he said, had earned a permanent place in the American soundtrack.

Stevie Wonder

The Motown Kid

Stevie Wonder drew on jazz and rhythm and blues to create a sound that was all his own—and became one of the best-selling musicians of all time. He had his first number one hit when he was just thirteen years old.

Stevie was born in Saginaw, Michigan, on May 13, 1950, as Steveland Hardaway Judkins. He arrived six weeks early and weighed less than four pounds. He spent more than a month in an incubator at the hospital, breathing oxygen-rich air into his underdeveloped lungs. The treatment helped him survive, but it also damaged his eyes. Today, premature babies are carefully monitored for this risk—but in those days, most doctors weren't aware of the danger that high oxygen levels posed to a newborn's vision.

Stevie's mom, Lula Hardaway, was devastated when the doctors said Stevie was blind. She was worried about how she would care for him; she already had Stevie's brothers, Milton and Calvin Junior, to look after, and she had very little money. And Lula had no support from her husband, Calvin Judkins. He was a heavy drinker who disappeared for weeks at a time—and when he was at home, he treated Lula very badly. The one good thing he did for Stevie was to give him bongo drums to play in his crib. Stevie loved them, and as he grew, so did his love of music. He would take pots and pans from the kitchen and bang on them with whatever he could find!

When Stevie was four, Lula moved the family to an apartment in Detroit. She'd hoped that Calvin might find work and start to treat her better, but he didn't change. Determined to build a life without him, she got a job at a fish market. She worked long hours, determined to move her family to a better neighborhood and into a house of their own. She hid some of the money she earned under her mattress so that Calvin wouldn't find it.

Lula didn't want Stevie to be treated differently because he was blind, and she tried not to be overprotective. Stevie liked playing behind their building, leaping from one storage bin to the next, or riding double on a bike with one of his brothers. Being blind, Stevie said, was normal for him, so he didn't think much about it. It did cause problems sometimes, though—like when he would step in dog poop in the backyard!

Stevie relied on his hearing a lot. "Your ears don't tell you everything," his mom used to warn him. "Beware of what's around you, child." But Stevie's hearing did tell him a great deal, and being a born entertainer, he sometimes used it to impress visitors. He would invite them to drop a coin on the table and then tell them whether it was a dime, a nickel, or a quarter by the sound it made.

When Stevie was six, Detroit got a new radio station that played the blues every Sunday night, and Stevie would listen for hours. His love of music was obvious to the people around him: the barber on his street gave Stevie a harmonica, a neighbor passed on her piano when she moved, and a community organization gave him a drum kit for Christmas.

When Stevie was eight, Lula took the family to a picnic in a park on Belle Isle. Bands played under the stars, and Stevie danced as close to the stage as he could. When the host of the show spotted him and held out the microphone, Stevie told him his name and listed some of his favorite musical acts. Then he added, "You know what else? I can play the drums." The next thing he knew, he was sitting behind the drum kit. As the band played, Stevie joined in, and after the song ended, he was given three quarters—it was his first paid performance!

When Stevie was ten, Lula moved the family to their first house, leaving Calvin behind. Stevie started attending the Fitzgerald School for the Blind, where he learned braille. He also made a new friend, John. Calling themselves "Stevie and John," the two boys jammed on the porch, John on his guitar and Stevie playing his harmonica. Soon they were playing on friends' porches as well as their own, and crowds of people often gathered on the sidewalk to listen.

John's cousin Ronnie White played with Smokey Robinson in a band called the Miracles. John asked Ronnie if he and his friend Stevie could come over to his house and play a few songs, and Ronnie agreed—just as a favor to family. When the boys arrived, Ronnie looked at Stevie and said, "I heard you're a pretty good singer." Never short on confidence, Stevie replied, "I can sing real good. I can sing badder than Smokey."

John strummed his guitar while Stevie sang a song he'd written, called "Lonely Boy," and added some harmonica as well. Ronnie was so impressed that he offered to take the boys for an audition with the famous Berry Gordy at the Motown Record Corporation the very next day. Lula had never heard of Berry Gordy, and she thought Stevie should focus on his education. Then again, she thought, maybe Stevie could make a little money to pay for college. She agreed that he could go to the audition if she came along too.

Ronnie drove them to the Motown studio on West Grand Boulevard in his white Cadillac. The company took its name from Detroit's nickname—Motor City, or Motor Town—and it would soon become famous for its many hit records. In fact, the blend of gospel, jazz, soul, and rhythm and blues that the studio produced became known as the Motown sound—or just Motown. But when Stevie Wonder showed up at the studio, it was just getting started.

Stevie sang, played the bongos, and blew on his harmonica—and within a few days, he and John had recording contracts. Stevie's contract was signed under the name Steveland Morris—Morris, Lula said, was a family name—but he would perform as Little Stevie Wonder.

It was around this time that Lula divorced Calvin and married Paul Hardaway, the father of her oldest son. They had a baby: Stevie's little sister, Renee. But Stevie was rarely at home; after school, he took the bus to Motown, where he'd stay until late at night.

His producer, Clarence Paul, became an important mentor to him. "Clarence was like a father, a brother, and a friend," Stevie said. Stevie was always in the studio, and he was always learning—but at times his pranks and know-it-all attitude annoyed people who were trying to get work done. Even Clarence admitted that Stevie could be "a pest."

Stevie's first album was released in 1962, when he was just twelve years old. It was called *The Jazz Soul of Little Stevie*, and it featured Stevie playing drums, piano, harmonica, and more—a virtual one-man band. His second album, a tribute to singer Ray Charles, was also released that fall—but neither album was a great success.

Stevie's breakthrough came later that year, and it happened not in the recording studio but in front of a live audience. In October 1962, he set off as part of the Motortown Revue, a concert lineup of acts that included the Miracles, the Supremes, the Temptations, Mary Wells, and Marvin Gaye. For nearly two months, they traveled in an old bus and several cars, performing nearly every night in more than thirty different cities. Some of those cities were in the South, where laws of segregation enforced discrimination against Black people. Stevie hadn't encountered racism like this before; the performers couldn't even eat in the same restaurants as white people or use the same bathrooms! At some of their concerts, police marked off separate areas for Black people in the audience using tape—and in Alabama, someone fired shots at their bus, narrowly missing the gas tank.

It was an exhausting trip, but Stevie had endless energy. Sometimes he'd play his bongos at two or three in the morning, until the others yelled at him to cut it out! He brought that same energy to his live performances—and one night at Chicago's Regal

Theater, it helped him make history. When Stevie played the song "Fingertips," he switched from his usual bongos to harmonica—and the crowd loved it. The recording was released in 1963, as an album called *Recorded Live: The 12 Year Old Genius.* It was the first Motown album to reach the top of the Billboard charts, and Stevie Wonder set a record as the youngest artist to reach that number-one spot.

Stevie went on to become Motown's best-selling solo artist and one of the world's best-selling musical artists of all time, with a career that included dozens of hit songs and a record-setting twenty-five Grammy Awards. He is also known for his activism and concern for social issues, using his music to raise funds and draw attention to issues such as disability rights, poverty, hunger, and homelessness.

Prince

A Joyous Sound

Prince has been called the greatest musical talent of his generation. On his debut album, he not only sang but also played all the instruments himself—twenty-seven different ones!

Both sides of Prince's family came from Louisiana. His father, John Lewis Nelson, was a jazz pianist and songwriter who had moved north to Minneapolis. There, he adopted the stage name Prince Rogers and started a band called the Prince Rogers Trio. Prince's mother, Mattie Della, was the group's jazz singer. They both had children from previous marriages: Mattie had a son, Alfred Jackson, and John had four children.

John and Mattie married in 1957, and their son was born the following year, on June 7, 1958, at Mount Sinai Hospital in Minneapolis. They named him Prince Rogers Nelson, after his father's stage name. When Prince was nearly two, his sister, Tyka, was born.

Prince later said that his very first memory was of his mother smiling at him. He said you could tell she was smiling just by looking into her eyes. His earliest memories also included his father playing piano, which he said was "a joyous sound." He remembered watching his father's fingers on the keys and desperately wanting to be able to play too.

Sometimes his mother and father would get dressed up and go out for a night on the town. Prince loved watching them get ready. "My parents were beautiful," he said. His mother's jewelry, gloves, and hat matched, and his father's suits were immaculate; each shirt had a matching tie, and his cuff links and rings sparkled. "Whenever they were happy with one another all was right [in] the world," he later wrote.

Ooooh!

After they left, it was Prince's turn to dress up and pretend. He was an imaginative child, and in his fantasy world, he sometimes lived on a mountain or a cloud, or in an underwater cave. His favorite book was *Harold and the Purple Crayon*, the story of a boy whose drawings come to life. "Prince loved 'pretend,'" his mother said.

He also dreamed of having secret flying abilities and would rush home from school to watch Superman on television. But Superman, like all the superheroes he saw on TV, was white. "That affects your self-image when you're black and watching white heroes," he said.

Prince's parents were Seventh-day Adventists, and the family went to church regularly. To Prince, the church service seemed to go on forever. They'd stop at the bakery on the way home too, and Prince would be in the back of the car, impatiently asking, "Are we there yet?" He just wanted to get home to watch *The Wizard of Oz*. He particularly loved the song "Over the Rainbow."

When Prince was five, he started riding the bus to a mostly white elementary school, where he often experienced racism. "I went to school with the rich kids who didn't like having me there," he said. Prince's teachers didn't want to call him Prince, although it was his legal name. "They thought it wasn't fit for a name," he said. "So they used Skipper instead." It was a nickname his mother had given him, and it stayed with him throughout his childhood.

Prince's father, John, played music at night, but during the day he worked at Honeywell as a plastics molder. He and Prince had a complicated relationship:

John was a hero to his young son, who was in awe of his musical skills, but he could also be a bully and didn't like Prince touching his piano. At times he was physically abusive to Prince and his mother. Prince often heard his parents fighting, an experience he later described as "soul-crushing."

When Prince was seven, a lot of things changed: his family moved to another house, his father left, and his parents divorced. Prince said he was happy to see his father leave because now he could play the piano whenever he wanted. After the divorce, everyone seemed happier. Prince and Tyka still saw their dad; John would visit on the weekends and take them to church and for dinner afterward. Prince began to take a more serious interest in music and wrote his first song, "Funk Machine," on his father's piano.

Prince was smaller than most kids his age, but he wanted to stand out. Tyka convinced him to try tap dancing. She looked up to him and told him that he was good at everything. Believing her, he entered the school talent show. It was a disaster—he had no music to accompany his act, only the sound of his feet tapping away. When he finished, people applauded . . . but Prince was pretty sure they were just clapping because they were so glad he'd finally stopped!

The local record store, Dee's Record Shop, was one of his favorite places. He would ride his bike there, buy a record, then write out all the words to the songs. He didn't know how to read music, but he'd learned by listening, teaching himself the chords, and singing along with artists such as James Brown, Ray Charles, Smokey Robinson, and Aretha Franklin.

When Prince was twelve, his mother, now a social worker in the public school system, remarried. Prince didn't get along with his stepfather, so he left, moving in with his dad. Prince saw this as a chance to learn from John; although their relationship wasn't always an easy one, his father understood his passion for music and bought him his first guitar.

By this time, Prince was attending Bryant Junior High, but he was more interested in his music than his classwork. One of his teachers wrote in his report card that Prince had "fine skills and a clever, perceptive mind" but also observed that he didn't listen in class, pay attention to instructions, or complete his assignments. "Prince could be doing much better work than he is, even though it is already above average," she said.

It was in middle school that Prince reconnected with an old friend named André Cymone. They'd been friends when they were seven or eight, singing together in the church choir. Now in their early teens, they were both music lovers who sometimes felt like outsiders, and they bonded quickly. When Prince was fourteen, he moved in with André and his family, and the two teenagers formed their first band.

In junior high, Prince impressed everyone with his basketball skills, but at Central High School, he soon ran into obstacles. He was just five feet two inches tall, and although he was a talented player, the coach thought he was too short to continue with the team after his freshman year. Prince was furious. Even years later, he was convinced that if he'd been playing, the team would have won the state championships all three years.

But Prince made a strong impression on his high school music teacher, Mrs. Doepke. In class when she asked the kids what their musical interests were, Prince said, "I want to become a rock-and-roll star." She later remembered him as a very quiet and serious student who rarely laughed or smiled, and added that there wasn't much she could teach him: "He was so good; he knew how to play amazingly well." When he wanted to borrow a synthesizer from the school, she had to say no—it was against the rules. But in the evening, she brought the synthesizer to his house. She stayed until late, joining in and playing maracas and tambourine with Prince and the rest of his band.

By his sophomore year of high school, all Prince wanted to do was make music. He played local gigs at night and he loved it—almost as much as he hated getting up and going to school the next morning. When he graduated, he was seventeen and didn't know how to pursue his dream. He had no money. But he started writing songs more seriously, producing an incredible three or four new songs a day!

Prince was just nineteen when he signed his first record deal. He drew on jazz, soul, funk, hip-hop, rock, and new wave, creating a sound that was uniquely his own. Over the next seven years, he released six albums, and in 1984, his album *Purple Rain* shot to the top of the chart and stayed there for months. It was also the soundtrack for the movie *Purple Rain*, in which he starred. Prince went on to release many more successful albums—thirty-nine in total—and is one of the best-selling musicians of all time.

Sadly, Prince died from an accidental drug overdose when he was just fifty-seven years old—but he left a powerful legacy in both his music and his influence on other artists. Throughout his career, he supported and mentored many other musicians—including Janelle Monáe, Kendrick Lamar, and the legendary pop star Lizzo, who appeared on a Prince album long before she was famous.

Mariah Carey

Music in My Voice

Mariah Carey has been dubbed the "Songbird Supreme" because of her extraordinary five-octave vocal range, and her blend of rhythm and blues, soul, pop, and hip-hop has influenced a generation of singers. She grew up surrounded by music and learned to whistle before she could talk!

Mariah Carey's mother, Patricia Hickey, was an opera singer, and her father, Alfred Roy Carey, was an engineer. In the 1950s, when the two of them met and fell in love in New York City, there was still a great deal of racist opposition to interracial marriage. Alfred was Black, from an African American and Venezuelan American family. Patricia was white, from an Irish Catholic family, and her mother refused to accept her daughter's relationship.

Mariah was born in Huntington, on New York's Long Island, on March 27, 1969. She was the youngest of three kids; when she was born, her brother, Morgan, was nine years old and her sister, Allison, was seven. Their parents had faced racist discrimination and harassment—once, their neighbors even set fire to their car—and the stress took a toll on the family. Mariah's earliest memories were of yelling, and chaos, and of feeling alone and unsafe. "I was always so scared as a little girl," she said.

Music was Mariah's escape. "My father taught me to whistle before I could talk," she said. She loved listening to her mom singing, and by age three she was singing too. One day, when her mom was practicing an aria from an opera, Mariah sang it back to her in perfect Italian!

When Mariah was three, her parents divorced. Allison moved in with their dad, and Mariah and Morgan stayed with their mom. Because their mom had to work, Mariah was often left at home alone with her brother. But Morgan had no interest in babysitting his little sister. Instead, he would go out with friends, leaving Mariah home alone. She found it scary—

especially one night when she watched a television show about children being kidnapped!

Mariah moved many times, but the family stayed on Long Island. She grew up in in communities where most people were white—and where, because she had light skin and hair, people often assumed she was too. At preschool, when she used a brown crayon to draw her father, the teachers laughed at her and told her she'd used the wrong crayon. Fighting back tears, Mariah insisted that she had used the right crayon for her father, but she was hurt and confused.

Mariah's teenage siblings often left her feeling hurt and confused as well—especially at Christmas. Mariah and her mom prepared for the holiday, counting down the days on an Advent calendar, decorating, and singing Christmas carols together as they prepared a special meal. Unfortunately, Christmas dinners often ended with a fight. Mariah's brother and sister didn't get along with each other and Mariah felt they both resented her—but she couldn't understand why they always had to ruin Christmas! "I would sit there in the center of the chaos, crying," she remembered. "Wishing I could be somewhere safe and merry. Somewhere that felt like *Christmas*."

That wish came true when Mariah and her mom spent Christmas with her mom's friends Burt and Myron, who were like family to her. "Two of my favorite people were my guncles (gay uncles), Burt and Myron," Mariah later wrote. At Christmas, their cozy house was decorated and there was delicious food to eat. There was even their dog, Sparkle, to pet. Best of all, when Mariah sang, she had an enthusiastic audience.

Mariah's family didn't have much money, but because her mom taught singing, they always had a piano and Mariah got singing lessons at home. One day, her friend Maureen told her, "When you sing, it sounds like there are instruments with you. There's music all around your voice." It was an important moment for Mariah: she realized that her voice was special and that she could use it to make people feel good.

When Mariah was in third grade, she discovered the actress Marilyn Monroe. To Mariah, Marilyn looked like a queen. She hung a poster of Marilyn on her bedroom wall, so she could look at her before she fell asleep. As she read more about her, she discovered that the actress had grown up poor and had a difficult childhood. She had felt like an outsider—yet she had become famous! Perhaps Mariah could too.

Mariah already knew that she loved to sing. She also loved performing in school plays. When she was about ten, she attended a performing arts summer camp, playing one of the lead parts in *Fiddler on the Roof.* Her mom helped her practice her songs at home, accompanying her on the piano. When it came time for the opening night show, Mariah was filled with confidence: she knew she was good. The applause was thunderous.

Mariah often sang with her mother and her mother's musician friends. She learned songs by Ella Fitzgerald and studied her all-time favorite, Stevie Wonder. When she was eleven or twelve, her mom started taking her to a jazz club. Mariah felt more at home there, among the musicians, than she did at school.

In middle school, other kids teased Mariah for being poor. Their words hurt her, but she tried not to let it show. She wanted desperately to be part of a group of popular Irish girls. They all had blue eyes and would chant "Blue eyes rule!" Mariah liked her own dark eyes, but she wanted to fit in. Finally, the popular girls invited her to a sleepover. But that night, the girls surrounded her and began chanting racist taunts. Mariah was devastated by their betrayal and cruelty.

But outside of school, she was pursuing her goals. In seventh grade, she had her first professional recording session, doing background vocals in a small home studio. "It was when I began to discover . . . how to use my voice to build layers, like a painter," she said.

By the time Mariah started high school, she was writing songs and recording the background vocals for radio commercials. By age fifteen, she had her first regular gig recording song demos for a couple of older musicians. She was learning a lot, but she really wanted to record her own songs. It was hard to get people to take her seriously. Finally, Mariah got the chance she'd been waiting for: alone in the studio, she recorded a song she had written herself.

Soon she was driving into New York City for recording sessions. The other students at her school had no idea she was spending her nights recording music! "I didn't talk about it because I knew it would sound crazy," she said. She knew she could make it as a singer-songwriter, but she wasn't sure anyone else would believe it.

At seventeen, Mariah moved to New York City on her own. She was so broke that she often had to choose between breakfast and subway tokens; if she bought a bagel to eat, she'd have to walk. But she didn't give up. She found jobs to pay the bills, and she kept recording songs. "Music was my whole life," she said.

In 1990, Mariah's first album was released, becoming a best-selling album in the United States—and at twenty years old, she won Grammy Awards for Best New Artist and Best Female Pop Vocal Performance.

Over the next thirty years, Mariah released many more successful albums. One of her songs, "All I Want for Christmas Is You," became the best-selling holiday song by a female artist and led her fans to call her the Queen of Christmas. Three decades after it was first released, it still fills the airwaves every December!

Mariah has been a trailblazer in other ways as well: breaking barriers for women and people of color, using her platform to advocate for LGBTQ+ equality, creating opportunities for underserved youth, and speaking openly about her own struggles with bipolar disorder to help fight the stigma of mental illness.

Marvin Gaye, sometimes called the Prince of Motown, was a powerful influence within the world of music as well as beyond it: he wrote one of the best-known songs of the anti-war movement. Born in Washington, DC, he moved to Detroit and became a prolific singer and songwriter. His 1971 album, *What's Going On*, tells the story of a young man returning from the Vietnam War only to witness poverty, racism, and injustice at home. Many contemporary R&B artists name Marvin Gaye as an important influence.

Other R&B artists also helped spread messages of equality and justice—such as Sam Cooke, whose song "A Change Is Gonna Come" became a rallying cry for the civil rights movement. Written in 1964 after Sam was turned away from a whites-only hotel in Louisiana, it is now considered one of the greatest songs of all time. The Queen of Soul, Aretha Franklin, was also involved in the struggles for women's rights and civil rights. Her songs, including "Respect," have inspired generations of people.

Further Reading

Bibliography

There are many wonderful books about musicians, including autobiographies (books written by the person about their own life) and biographies (books about noteworthy people written by someone else). This is a list of some of the main sources used by the author in researching and writing this book.

PART 1

Cher

Cher and Jeff Coplon. *The First Time*. New York: Simon and Schuster, 1998.

Beyoncé

Greenidge, Kaitlyn. "Beyoncé's Evolution." *Harper's Bazaar*. August 10, 2021. https://www.harpersbazaar.com/culture/features /a37039502/beyonce-evolution-interview-2021.

Taraborrelli, J. Randy. *Becoming Beyoncé: The Untold Story*. New York: Grand Central Publishing, 2016.

Harry Styles

Smith, Sean. *Harry Styles: The Making of a Modern Man*. London: HarperCollins, 2021.

Taylor Swift

Newkey-Burden, Chas. *Taylor Swift Unauthorised: The Whole Story.* New York: HarperCollins, 2014.

Wilson, Lana, dir. *Miss Americana.* Tremolo Productions, 2020. Netflix.

PART 2

Louis Armstrong

Armstrong, Louis. *Satchmo: My Life in New Orleans.* New York: Da Capo Press, 1986. Originally published in 1954 by Prentice Hall (New York).

Bergreen, Laurence. *Louis Armstrong: An Extravagant Life.* New York: Broadway Books, 1997.

Ella Fitzgerald

Bernays, Paul, dir. *Ella Fitzgerald: First Lady of Song.* Legends series. BBC, 2007.

Nicholson, Stuart. *Ella Fitzgerald: A Biography of the First Lady of Jazz.* New York: Da Capo Press, 1995. Originally published in 1993 by MacMillan (New York).

Woodhead, Leslie, dir. *Ella Fitzgerald: Just One of Those Things.* Eagle Rock Film Productions, 2019. Netflix.

Glenn Gould

Bazzana, Kevin. *Wondrous Strange: The Life and Art of Glenn Gould.* New York: Oxford University Press, 2005.

Yo-Yo Ma

Blum, David. "Yo-Yo Ma's Musical Mind." *New Yorker*, April 23, 1989. https://www.newyorker.com/magazine/1989/05/01/yo-yo-ma-a-process-larger-than-oneself.

Ma, Marina, and John A. Rallo. *My Son, Yo-Yo*. Hong Kong: Chinese University of Hong Kong, 1995.

Whiting, Jim. *Yo-Yo Ma: A Biography*. Westport, CT: Greenwood Press, 2008.

PART 3

Paul McCartney

Norman, Philip. *Paul McCartney: The Life*. New York: Little, Brown and Company, 2016.

Joni Mitchell

Montagne, Renee. "The Music Midnight Makes: In Conversation with Joni Mitchell." NPR, December 9, 2014. www.npr.org/2014/12/09/369386571/the-music-midnight-makes-in-conversation-with-joni-mitchell.

Yaffe, David. *Reckless Daughter: A Portrait of Joni Mitchell*. Toronto: HarperCollins, 2017.

Bob Marley

Farley, Christopher. *Before the Legend: The Rise of Bob Marley*. Paperback ed. New York: Amistad, 2007.

Steffens, Roger. *So Much Things to Say: The Oral History of Bob Marley.* New York: W. W. Norton, 2017.

White, Timothy. *Catch a Fire: The Life of Bob Marley.* Revised ed. New York: Holt, 2006.

Dolly Parton

Parton, Dolly. *Dolly: My Life and Other Unfinished Business.* New York: Harper Collins, 1994.

PART 4

Diana Ross

Taraborrelli, J. Randy. *Diana Ross: A Biography.* Kindle ed. New York: Citadel, 2014.

Stevie Wonder

Love, Dennis, and Stacy Brown. *Blind Faith: The Miraculous Journey of Lula Hardaway, Stevie Wonder's Mother.* New York: Simon and Schuster, 2002.

Ribowsky, Mark. *Signed, Sealed, Delivered: The Soulful Journey of Stevie Wonder.* Hoboken, NJ: John Wiley and Sons, 2010.

Prince

Karlen, Neal. *This Thing Called Life: Prince's Odyssey On and Off the Record.* New York: St. Martin's Press, 2020.

Prince. *The Beautiful Ones.* Edited by Dan Piepenbring. New York: Random House, 2019.

Mariah Carey

Carey, Mariah, and Michaela Angela Davis. *The Meaning of Mariah Carey.* New York: St. Martin's Griffin, 2020.

Index

M

N

S

Paul McCartney, 114–24; Prince, 10, 12, 38, 184–95; Taylor Swift, 11, 12, 51–62

T

U

V

They're Little Kids with Big Dreams . . . and Big Problems!

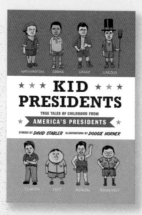

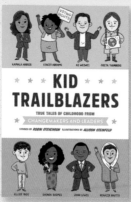

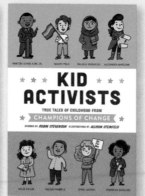